F. R. LEAVIS

D0713994

F. R. Leavis is a landmark figure in twentieth-century literary criticism and theory. His outspoken and confrontational work has often divided opinion and continues to generate interest as students and critics revisit his highly influential texts.

Looking closely at a representative selection of Leavis's work, Richard Storer outlines his thinking on key topics such as:

- Literary theory, 'criticism' and culture
- Canon formation
- Modernism
- Close reading
- Higher education.

Exploring the responses and engaging with the controversies generated by Leavis's work, this clear, authoritative guide highlights how Leavis remains of critical significance to twenty-first-century study of literature and culture.

Richard Storer is Associate Principal Lecturer and Director of BA Programmes in English at Leeds Trinity and All Saints, an accredited college of the University of Leeds. His publications include *F. R. Leavis: Essays and Documents* (co-edited with Ian MacKillop, 1995).

ROUTLEDGE CRITICAL THINKERS

Series Editor: Robert Eaglestone, Royal Holloway, University of London

Routledge Critical Thinkers is a series of accessible introductions to key figures in contemporary critical thought.

With a unique focus on historical and intellectual contexts, the volumes in this series examine important theorists':

- significance
- motivation
- key ideas and their sources
- impact on other thinkers

Concluding with extensively annotated guides to further reading, *Routledge Critical Thinkers* are the student's passport to today's most exciting critical thought.

Also available in the series:

Louis Althusser by Luke Ferretter
Roland Barthes by Graham Allen
Jean Baudrillard by Richard J. Lane
Simone de Beauvoir by Ursula Tidd
Homi K. Bhabha by David Huddart
Maurice Blanchot by Ullrich Haase and William Large
Judith Butler by Sara Salih
Gilles Deleuze by Claire Colebrook
Jacques Derrida by Nicholas Royle
Michel Foucault by Sara Mills
Sigmund Freud by Pamela Thurschwell
Antonio Gramsci by Steve Jones
Stephen Greenblatt by Mark Robson
Stuart Hall by James Procter
Martin Heidegger by Timothy Clark
Fredric Jameson by Adam Roberts
Jean-François Lyotard by Simon Malpas
Jacques Lacan by Sean Homer
Emmanuel Levinas by Seán Hand
Julia Kristeva by Noëlle McAfee

For further information on this series visit:
www.routledgeliterature.com/books/series

F. R. LEAVIS

Richard Storer

Routledge
Taylor & Francis Group

LONDON AND NEW YORK

First edition published 2009 by Routledge
2 Park Square, Milton Park, Abingdon, Oxon OX14 4RN

Simultaneously published in the USA and Canada
by Routledge
711 Third Avenue, New York, NY 10017, USA

*Routledge is an imprint of the Taylor & Francis Group, an
informa business*

© 2009 Richard Storer

Typeset in Series Design Selected by Taylor & Francis Books

British Library Cataloguing in Publication Data
A catalogue record for this book is available from the
British Library

Library of Congress Cataloging in Publication Data
Storer, Richard.
    F.R. Leavis / by Richard Storer. – 1st ed.
        p. cm. – (Routledge critical thinkers)
    Includes bibliographical references and index.
    1. Leavis, F. R. (Frank Raymond), 1895-1978. 2. English
literature–History and criticism–Theory, etc. 3. Criticism–
England–History–20th century. I. Title.
    PR55.L43S76 2009
    801′.95092–dc22
    2009002261
                                              200803909

ISBN10: 0-415-36416-7 (hbk)
ISBN10: 0-415-36417-5 (pbk)
ISBN10: 0-203-01535-5 (ebk)

ISBN13: 978-0-415-36416-4 (hbk)
ISBN13: 978-0-415-36417-1 (pbk)
ISBN13: 978-0-203-01535-3 (ebk)

CONTENTS

SERIES EDITOR'S
PREFACE

The books in this series offer introductions to major critical thinkers who have influenced literary studies and the humanities. The *Routledge Critical Thinkers* series provides the books you can turn to first when a new name or concept appears in your studies.

Each book will equip you to approach a key thinker's original texts by explaining their key ideas, putting then into context and, perhaps most importantly, showing you why this thinker is considered to be significant. The emphasis is on concise, clearly written guides which do not presuppose a specialist knowledge. Although the focus is on particular figures, the series stresses that no critical thinker ever existed in a vacuum but, instead, emerged from a broader intellectual, cultural and social history. Finally, these books will act as a bridge between you and the thinkers' original texts: not replacing them but rather complementing what they wrote. In some cases, volumes consider small clusters of thinkers, working in the same area, developing similar ideas or influencing each other.

These books are necessary for a number of reasons. In his 1997 autobiography, *Not Entitled*, the literary critic Frank Kermode wrote of a time in the 1960s:

> On beautiful summer lawns, young people lay together all night, recovering from their daytime exertions and listening to a troupe of Balinese musicians.

> Under their blankets or their sleeping bags, they would chat drowsily about the gurus of the time … What they repeated was largely hearsay; hence my lunchtime suggestion, quite impromptu, for a series of short, very cheap books offering authoritative but intelligible introductions to such figures.

There is still a need for 'authoritative and intelligible introductions'. But this series reflects a different world from the 1960s. New thinkers have emerged and the reputations of others have risen and fallen, as new research has developed. New methodologies and challenging ideas have spread through the arts and humanities. The study of literature is no longer – if it ever was – simply the study and evaluation of poems, novels and plays. It is also the study of ideas, issues and difficulties which arise in any literary text and in its interpretation. Other arts and humanities subjects have changed in analogous ways.

With these changes, new problems have emerged. The ideas and issues behind these radical changes in the humanities are often presented without reference to wider contexts or as theories which you can simply 'add on' to the texts you read. Certainly, there's nothing wrong with picking out selected ideas or using what comes to hand – indeed, some thinkers have argued that this is, in fact, all we can do. However, it is sometimes forgotten that each new idea comes from the pattern and development of somebody's thought and it is important to study the range and context of their ideas. Against theories 'floating in space', the *Routledge Critical Thinkers* series places key thinkers and their ideas firmly back in their contexts.

More than this, these books reflect the need to go back to the thinkers' own texts and ideas. Every interpretation of an idea, even the most seemingly innocent one, offers you its own 'spin', implicitly or explicitly. To read only books on a thinker, rather than texts by that thinker, is to deny yourself a chance of making up your own mind. Sometimes what makes a significant figure's work hard to approach is not so much its style or the content as the feeling of not knowing where to start. The purpose of these books is to give you a 'way in' by offering an accessible overview of these thinkers' ideas and works and by guiding your further reading, starting with each thinker's own texts. To use a metaphor from the philosopher Ludwig Wittgenstein (1889–1951), these books are ladders, to be thrown away after you have climbed to the next level. Not only, then, do they equip you to approach new ideas, but also they empower you, by leading you back to the theorist's own texts and encouraging you to develop your own informed opinions.

Finally, these books are necessary because, just as intellectual needs have changed, the education systems around the world – the contexts in which introductory books are usually read – have changed radically, too. What was suitable for the minority higher education systems of the 1960s is not suitable for the larger, wider, more diverse, high technology education systems of the twenty-first century. These changes call not just for new, up-to-date introductions but new methods of presentation. The presentational aspects of *Routledge Critical Thinkers* have been developed with today's students in mind.

Each book in the series has a similar structure. They begin with a section offering an overview of the life and ideas of the featured thinkers and explain why they are important. The central section of each book discusses the thinkers' key ideas, their context, evolution, and reception; with the books that deal with more than one thinker, they also explain and explore the influence of each on each. The volumes conclude with a survey of the impact of the thinker or thinkers, outlining how their ideas have been taken up and developed by others. In addition, there is a detailed final section suggesting and describing books for further reading. This is not a 'tacked-on' section but an integral part of each volume. In the first part of this section you will find brief descriptions of the thinkers' key works, then, following this, information on the most useful critical works and, in some cases, on relevant websites. This section will guide you in your reading, enabling you to follow your interests and develop your own projects. Throughout each book, references are given in what is known as the Harvard system (the author and the date of a work cited are given in the text and you can look up the full details in the bibliography at the back). This offers a lot of information in very little space. The books also explain technical terms and use boxes to describe events or ideas in more detail, away from the main emphasis of the discussion. Boxes are also used at times to highlight definitions of terms frequently used or coined by a thinker. In this way, the boxes serve as a kind of glossary, easily identified when flicking through the book.

The thinkers in the series are 'critical' for three reasons. First, they are examined in the light of subjects which involve criticism: principally literary studies or English and cultural studies, but also other disciplines which rely on the criticism of books, ideas, theories and unquestioned assumptions. Second, they are critical because studying their work will provide you with a 'tool kit' for your own informed critical reading and thought, which will make you critical. Third, these thinkers are critical because they are crucially important: they deal with ideas and questions which can overturn conventional under-standings of the world, of texts, of everything we take for granted, leaving us with a deeper understanding of what we already knew and with new ideas.

No introduction can tell you everything. However, by offering a way into critical thinking, this series hopes to begin to engage you in an activity which is productive, constructive and potentially life-changing.

ACKNOWLEDGEMENTS

I would very much like to thank Robert Eaglestone, the series editor, for his invitation to write this book; and for his encouragement and positive advice at every stage. I would also like to thank Chris Joyce, William Baker and William E. Cain for their helpful comments at an early stage. I am grateful to my colleagues in the Department of Humanities at Leeds Trinity and All Saints, who have been a constant source of inspiration and support; I would particularly like to thank Joyce Simpson and Clare Pickles for their generous practical help at certain key stages. Most of all I thank my wife and daughters for their patience and for their cheerful and loving support throughout the whole process.

I would like to take this opportunity to acknowledge how much I owe to the late Ian MacKillop, my former research supervisor and also co-editor with me of an earlier Leavis book. He died before I had written one word of this book, but I could not have either started or finished it without the benefit of all that I learned from working with Ian over the years before.

ABBREVIATIONS

For references to books by F. R. Leavis, and two books about him, I have used the abbreviations listed below. Full bibliographical details for all Leavis's books are given in the final chapter ('Further Reading'). For references to other texts by Leavis, and texts by other authors, full details are given in 'Works Cited'.

AK	*'Anna Karenina' and Other Essays* (1967)
CAP	[ed. G. Singh] *The Critic as Anti-Philosopher: Essays and Papers* (1982)
CE	[with Denys Thompson] *Culture and Environment* (1933)
DHLN	*D. H. Lawrence: Novelist* (1955)
DN	[with Q. D. Leavis] *Dickens the Novelist* (1970)
EU	*Education and the University* (1943)
ELTU	*English Literature in Our Time and the University* (1969)
FC	*For Continuity* (1933)
GS	G. Singh, *F. R. Leavis: A Literary Biography* (1995)
GT	*The Great Tradition: George Eliot, Henry James, Joseph Conrad* (1948)
IM	Ian MacKillop, *F. R. Leavis: A Life in Criticism* (1995)
LA	[with Q. D. Leavis] *Lectures in America* (1969)
LC	[ed. John Tasker] *Letters in Criticism* (1974)
LP	*The Living Principle: 'English' as a Discipline of Thought* (1975)

NBEP	*New Bearings in English Poetry: A Study of the Con-temporary Situation* (1932)
NSMS	*Nor Shall My Sword: Essays in Pluralism, Compassion and Social Hope* (1972)
TCP	*The Common Pursuit* (1952)
RV	*Revaluation: Tradition and Development in English Poetry* (1936)
VC	[ed. G. Singh] *Valuation in Criticism and Other Essays* (1986)

WHY LEAVIS?

Any great creative writer who has not had his due is a power for life wasted.

F. R. (Frank Raymond) Leavis (1895–1978) was a writer and university teacher, based in Cambridge, England, who was active from the 1920s to the 1970s.

His interest was in English literature and its relation to modern culture; and he is often described as one of the most important figures in English literary studies in the twentieth century. Why he was important, and what this description could mean, is something that this book as a whole will explore. The first thing it usually means is that during his lifetime Leavis was very influential. His career began at an exciting time for literary studies, and he is often grouped with other writers and teachers who played a part in this. But Leavis's influence was more concentrated, more carefully sustained, and in the end more widely disseminated, than that of any of his contemporaries. It was felt at first in the reading of English poetry, but then extended to the study of the English novel as well. It was not just focused on the study of literature but on the cultural and educational conditions within which literature was studied. It worked through his teaching and lecturing, but also through *Scrutiny*, the Cambridge-based quarterly journal that ran between 1932 and 1953, of which Leavis was the chief editor; and also through over twenty books which he either wrote or edited.

Leavis succeeded in convincing his students and readers that studying literature mattered for the future of humanity – and no other twentieth-century writer has been quite so successful in doing this as Leavis. His profile in America was always lower, though he was well known, but in the British context it is hard to describe the psychological hold Leavis had over generations of students, teachers and writers. 'Influence' does not really say enough, because Leavis was a controversial figure who divided opinion as much as he shaped it, and he was resented and disliked almost as much as he was respected and admired. One reason for this is that he was a genuinely radical public figure, prepared to make uncompromising statements of his views even at the cost of embarrassing more moderate supporters who broadly shared those views. Leavis was also radical in the sense that he exposed the roots of the thinking on which the discussion of literature is based. He raised questions about why we read, how we should read, what reading has got to do with life – questions which we all have to address as long as we think it is worthwhile to pick up a book. And he did not just ask these questions but argued quite forcefully for what he thought the answers should be. This book provides an outline of Leavis's answers, as well as his questions and their context. The key term which focuses them all is the one that I have deliberately avoided using up to now: criticism.

THE FUNCTION OF CRITICISM

'Critic' is the word most often used to describe Leavis. It was one that he himself frequently used; the epitaph 'teacher and critic' was even inscribed on his memorial stone after his cremation. But to introduce Leavis as 'critic' is to suggest that everyone knows what a 'critic' is and does, whereas one of the interesting things about Leavis is the way his career challenges preconceptions about the role of the critic, and the relation of 'criticism' to other kinds of writing.

Leavis's idea of what criticism is and does, and why it matters, is perhaps summed up in the statement I put at the beginning of this chapter: 'any great creative writer who has not had his due is a power for life wasted' (*DHLN* 15). There are lots of things about this for-mulation we might find questionable: the conventional assumptions behind that *his*, for example; or the economic metaphors (*had his due*, *wasted*) which Leavis relies on very heavily in all his writing; or the phrase *power for life*, which was probably intended to evoke religious associations but today looks more like the marketing slogan for an energy supplier. But we can surely still recognise the appeal of what Leavis is saying – that there is such a thing as great creative writing, that it has the potential to make a positive contribution to the way human life is lived, and that realising this potential is a process towards which we can feel a certain responsibility. Anyone who has ever expressed an opinion about a literary text they value, and thought their opinion worth defending, has in some sense subscribed to the ideal Leavis is articulating. No matter how sophisticated the discourses of literary studies become, it is unlikely this basic impulse to affirm and articulate value can ever be repressed.

I have quoted the 'power for life' phrase, of course, not just because it provides a good summary of Leavis's attitude to criticism, but because it seems to me it can also be applied to Leavis himself. 'Critical' writing is often distinguished from 'creative' writing, with the implication that 'criticism' is the more sterile, secondary mode. A related implication is that the most authoritative criticism is that which is informed by experience of being a creative writer. Here it is worth mentioning some of the other critics with whom Leavis is often associated: T. S. Eliot (1888–1965); the 'Cambridge critics' I. A. Richards (1893–1979) and William Empson (1906–84); and the more diffuse American group, including John Crowe Ransom (1888–1974), often identified as the 'New Critics'. Most of these critics were also poets. Eliot, Empson and Richards all published their own poetry (though to very different degrees of critical acclaim) as well as writing about the work of others – and the same is true of many of the 'New Critics'. But F. R. Leavis offers no such 'creative' alias. He did not (so far as is known) write poems, stories or plays. He only really had one genre of writing in his repertoire – the essay – and he was not even particularly radically innovative, in terms of form or subject matter, in his use of this. To describe Leavis as 'critic', then, seems to confine him to a narrow and essentially secondary role. But it could be argued that by abstaining so completely from the 'creative' Leavis actually challenges the conventional understanding of the different functions of 'creative' and 'critical'. Criticism for Leavis *was* creative writing: the careful selection of words to bring about shared understanding. Leavis thus provides a rather different model for creativity from that with which we are familiar.

Another uncertainty about 'criticism' is *where* exactly it belongs. Leavis grew up with the convention that 'criticism' was an essentially public discourse: a form of journalism sustained by the existence of print media – newspapers, weekly magazines, 'little magazines', and so on. He seems to have retained this way of thinking about 'criticism' throughout his career, while regarding the 'literary world' which was responsible for criticism as increasingly compromised and degraded by commercial pressures and personal irresponsibility. At the same time, during Leavis's lifetime, a huge expansion took place in criticism as something that goes on in universities, particularly in the study of literature. There are no degree programmes in 'criticism' as such, but the word 'critical' is everywhere in academic discourse – 'critical approaches', 'critical theory', 'critical debate', 'critical thinking', 'critical literacy'. It is probably true to say that many academics think of their own writing, however specialised, as 'criticism' – and think of 'criticism' in this sense as now belonging to the academy rather than to any more public or commercial forum. Leavis's solution to the problem of what he saw as a compromised 'literary world' was that 'the university' should take over some of its functions and, at the same time, in so doing – in becoming an effective centre of 'criticism' – detach itself from some of its more 'academic' characteristics, which he saw as equally undesirable. Leavis believed, then, that criticism should be located between the academic and the journalistic, and that to speak in that space was the most important modern function of the university. In trying to understand what he believed criticism should be, then, we cannot avoid Leavis's ideas about what a university should be: indeed these ideas can still speak quite prophetically, as I suggest later, to the condition of higher education in the twenty-first century.

The chapter title 'Why Leavis?' actually echoes the title of an essay Leavis published early in his career, 'Why Universities?' (Leavis 1934). It is quite well known that Leavis believed 'English' should be thought of as the 'central' subject in a modern university. Fellow academics have often regarded this as an unhelpful or embarrassing claim – and it is doubtful whether it has ever figured in the 'corporate plan' or prospectus of any academic institution. Can any sense be made of it now? What did Leavis really mean? All he was really claiming, perhaps, was that in modern industrial civilisation the kind of human wisdom articulated in great literary texts should be regarded as having some authority; and no other discourse (scientific or social-scientific) should be regarded as having *more* authority. It is the metaphor of the 'centre' which presents a sticking-point; and there is no doubt of its importance – its centrality, we might say – to Leavis. Leavis is central to the history of 'English' – or rather the history of 'English' as a form of *criticism* – in the sense that he represents more dramatically than any other figure the idea that criticism should be about *centres*. In an often-quoted passage from an early essay Leavis wrote about the role of the intelligent critic:

> Upon this minority depends our power of profiting by the finest human experience of the past; they keep alive the subtlest and most perishable parts of human tradition. Upon them depend the implicit standards that order the finer living of an age, the sense that this is worth more than that, this rather than that is the direction in which to go, *that the centre is here rather than there* …
>
> (*FC* 15; my italics)

This passage is often cited as an example of an elitism implicit in Leavis's thinking (the arbitrary appropriation by 'this minority' of authority over what is 'finest' and 'subtlest' and over what represents 'human tradition'). This is certainly a significant problem with Leavis's model (though as Leavis himself pointed out, the assertion of values by an elite, if it is to be perceived as a problem, is actually a problem with most models of social organisation (see *NSMS* 209–13)). But it is equally important to keep sight of what 'centre' actually stands for here, which is shared values. In arguing that 'the centre is here rather than there' the critic is really suggesting: isn't this what we both think? The role of the critic is to maintain community.

'A BATTLE TO BE FOUGHT EVERYWHERE'

My emphases so far on creativity, sharing, and community, as concepts to be associated with Leavis, must seem quite perverse to anyone familiar with his reputation, which is traditionally that of a 'rancorous dogmatist' (Selden 1989: 19). 'Rancorous' is just one item in a long list that could be compiled of negative terms that have been applied to Leavis which make him a byword for a destructive or unacceptably hostile approach to criticism: violent, vindictive, vituperative, belligerent, spiteful, ferocious, defamatory …; in one Cultural Studies textbook Leavis is even imagined issuing death threats to people who do not share his views (Hawkins 1990: xiv). The perception behind these caricatures is that in some sense Leavis did not observe the rules of engagement. 'Criticism' is about pointing out weaknesses, it is implied, but Leavis goes too far. 'I can't trust him' Lord Snow wrote in 1970, explaining why he would not respond directly to a lecture in which Leavis had described him as 'intellectually as undistinguished as it is possible to be' (Snow 1970: 737; *NSMS* 42)

It is important to note that this image of Leavis as uncivilised rebel is in many ways misleading. First, the image of Leavis lashing out intemperately, like a bad-tempered blogger, is simply wrong. The reason his attacks were noticed and remembered is not because they were unusually aggressive but because they were so crushingly deliberate. There is little sense of personal animus in Leavis's polemical prose; rather, he cultivated the 'impersonal' – the sense that his judgements were inevitable and only articulated what everyone already knew. Again, the prevailing impression of Leavis as habitually destructive and negative is also wrong. He was radical but he was also in many ways conservative; and far from being a fierce individualist the recurring emphasis in his writing is on an appeal to *shared* values: 'Criticism, with all it stands for, is collaborative and creative. Mere lonely intransigence is barren' (*LC* 74). The term 'belligerent' is right, however, in its proper sense, not of someone mindlessly picking fights with innocent passers-by but of someone who thought of himself as constantly and intently *waging war*. Military metaphors turn up frequently in Leavis's writings, particularly towards the end of his career – often on subjects which seem fairly uncontroversial. 'There is a battle to be fought everywhere' he wrote in the early 1960s – in a contribution to a discussion on the best way to train postgraduate research students (*ELTU* 194).

Where did Leavis get this sense of himself as constantly embattled? And who or what exactly was the enemy? One could easily sum up Leavis's life in much less dramatic terms. He was born and educated in Cambridge, where his father was a successful local businessman, the proprietor of several shops selling pianos and other musical instruments. He lived almost the whole of his life in Cambridge. The most outwardly dramatic episode in his life, paradoxically, is distinguished by its *non*-combatant nature. During the First World War, which broke out just before Leavis started at Cambridge University in 1914, he did not serve in the armed forces but as an orderly on a hospital train, in France, operated by the non-combatant Friends Ambulance Unit. There are other later circumstances which have often been taken to explain his sense of himself as at odds with the world – particularly the setbacks which he encountered in trying to establish himself within the university (I examine these circumstances in more detail in Chapter 7). It may also have had something to do with Leavis's strong identification with the puritan or non-conformist tradition in English culture. There is no doubt that, wherever it came from, the 'embattled' stance ran deep in Leavis's thinking (which in his case also means feeling) about everything; and, whether he chose it or it chose him, it was a mode he found productive for the performance of his thinking. As his biographer Ian MacKillop notes, Leavis referred to the numerous lectures he gave in the 1960s and 1970s as 'field-performances' (*IM 374*) – a figure of speech which appropriately combines the suggestion of military role-play (field as in battle-field) with awareness that the 'battle' *was* nevertheless essentially a performance, directed towards an audience as much as towards the perceived enemy. If he had not written in this way, but in the more accommodating style which most of us find more congenial most of the time, we probably would not be asking 'Why Leavis?' now. There is a dramatic edge to Leavis's writing which makes it more memorable.

READING LEAVIS

Compared to many of the critical thinkers that students are often encouraged to engage with, Leavis's writing is not really that difficult to read. He does not go in for ostentatious wordplay or for the spatial and architectural metaphors (*space, site, location, margin, structure*, etc.) which are a stylistic feature of much contemporary critical theory (*centre* of course is one important exception). Nor does he appear to use a particularly specialised vocabulary. A few obscure jargon terms, such as *ahnung* and *nisus*, do start to appear in his later writing and require some explanation, but Leavis is careful to provide this (*LP 62*). The words which seem to be doing most work in his writing, however, are often everyday words which seem almost too unsophisticated for their context: words like *blank, plain, there, real, point, done, life*.

Reading Leavis for the first time, nevertheless, you may well find his distinctive written style somewhat impenetrable, and wonder why he does not get to the point more directly. His style is notoriously indirect. Leavis's habit of retreating into more and more parentheses and sub-clauses before he commits himself to completing a sentence seems partly modelled on the style of the American novelist Henry James whom he particularly admired. An earlier model is provided by the English Renaissance poet John Donne, particularly a passage which Leavis admired and quoted several times in different contexts:

> On a huge hill,
> Cragged and steep, Truth stands, and he that will
> Reach her, about must, and about must go:
> And what the hill's suddenness resists, win so ...

Leavis described this as the 'Shakespearian use of English ... The words seem to do what they say' (*RV* 55); meaning that as one attempts to track the sense of the sentence across the lines of verse the satisfaction of reaching a conclusion is repeatedly deferred, may even seem unobtainable, then is suddenly delivered – rather like the attempt to reach the summit of a hill in Donne's figure of speech. As a way of accounting for how language works, the idea that words can in fact *do* what they *say* is highly problematic, of course, and has been stigmatised as the 'enactment fallacy' (see Barry 1995: 20; Bell 1988: 42). But this does not detract from the point that Leavis intended *his* words to do what Donne describes. There is a lot of the 'about must, and about must go' about the movement of his prose, but there are also moments of memorable directness which are all the more powerful in their effect for the sense of deliberation that has preceded them. Leavis's style is not designed to deliver instant lucidity, but works deliberately towards more hard-won insight. (For a good analysis of this style and the way it mixes 'the vocabulary of taste with the vocabulary of effort', see Mulhern 1995.)

In the 1930s the Czech critic René Wellek invented a way of summarising Leavis's thinking which has been widely used since. He presented Leavis with a list of all the evaluative terms and phrases which he felt his criticism relied on, and then suggested that Leavis must agree with this summary as all the terms were 'tags' copied word for word from Leavis's essays. As one reads Leavis, one is constantly tempted to 'tag' his thinking in the same way, and it is impossible to avoid foregrounding certain terms or quoting 'key' passages as one goes on. It is important to sound a note of caution about this method, however. The word 'tag' has interesting connotations now of control and surveillance: we 'tag' endangered species and delinquent youths (it was even suggested in the UK recently that we should 'tag' absent-minded senior citizens) and there is something of this in Wellek's method: isolating what seem to be Leavis's key terms somehow *contains* his discourse. But Leavis did not agree exactly with the summary Wellek proposed, for the good reason that it did not adequately explain how he intended his words to work.

To get a proper sense of how Leavis's terms are intended to work, it is not essential to read whole books at a time. Most of the chapters in Leavis's books were originally written as essays for publication in journals or for a public lecture; and with a strategic purpose in that context. So although the books have a logic of their own, and are important because through them Leavis reached a larger audience, one can still learn a lot about Leavis from reading a few essays, since each one focuses the 'battle to be fought everywhere'. It is important to read the *whole* essay in each case, however. I have included in the 'Further Reading' chapter of this book a list of the essays I recommend for this purpose.

'MONSTROUS INDUSTRY': ABOUT THIS BOOK

This book is organised around topics which feature prominently in Leavis's writings and also in writing about him. Students are likely to come across references to Leavis, detailed or passing, in the context of discussions of any of the following: literary theory, culture, modernism, canon-forming, close reading, and higher education; so these are the topics for the 'Key Ideas' Chapters 2–7. Chapter 1 provides a more general framework for thinking about Leavis by thinking about some of the categories into which he is often put, and also providing a further outline of his career and development. Chapter 8, on 'Life', covers a topic which is peculiarly associated with Leavis. The final two chapters, in keeping with the format for this series, consider the influence of Leavis and provide detailed advice on further reading of and about him.

Although I have thus organised this book with the student in mind, it would be particularly ironic if a book on Leavis addressed only the student and not any wider readership. So I have tried as much as possible to make this a book which will interest other readers, though I recognise some aspects of it may also irritate them. Leavis himself was fairly unequivocal on what he thought of introductory 'aids to study', referring to 'the immense, the monstrous, industry of book-manufacture addressed to the vast new student-populace' and accusing the authors of 'blank ignorance of what the profitable study of literature is like' (*LP* 24). He never knew of this particular book series, of course, though there is good reason to believe that when he made this remark he was thinking specifically of the popular series, edited by Frank Kermode in the 1970s, which is indirectly cited as a model in the Series Editor's Preface to this book. But perhaps there is a sense in which a book on Leavis *ought* to be 'monstrous', because the image of Leavis himself was and is 'monstrous' in lots of ways familiar from the gothic genre: transgressive, excessive, forceful, feared, despised, often warned against, routinely attacked … One anonymous early attack on Leavis, complaining that his criticism was made up of incongruously combined elements from different sources, specifically conjured the image of the kind of monster known as a *chimera*: 'Eliot's head and Lawrence's tail do not fit together at all' ('Ille Ego' 1933: 282). The whole point about studying monsters, of course, and the whole reason they fascinate or repel, is what they reveal to us about ourselves and our sense of what we are and what we are not. This is one more reason, I think, why Leavis is still worth reading and reading about. In determining what we think of him, and what he thought, we are inevitably reflecting on what we think 'the profitable study of litera-ture is like' – what it has been, what it is, what it is not, and what it should be.

KEY IDEAS

1

'WHAT IS LEAVIS'?

It's an odd question, but a good one – and not my own but first asked by the American modernist poet Ezra Pound in the early 1930s: 'What is Leavis? He sent me his Primer' (Paige 1950: 246). Like almost everyone else in the world beyond Cambridge at the time, Pound had never heard of Leavis, and was surprised to have received a pamphlet from him, cheekily entitled *How to Teach Reading: A Primer for Ezra Pound*. He probably meant '*Who* is Leavis?' of course, but 'What is Leavis?' raises questions more relevant to the focus of this book. What kind of thinker is Leavis? Is there a tradition to which he belongs, or a category which we can use to make sense of him? What is the most relevant way to introduce him

This chapter builds on the first chapter by exploring three related but different ways in which Pound's question can be (and often has been) answered. First it locates Leavis (where he explicitly located himself) in the *Arnoldian* tradition. Then it considers what it means to identify Leavis as a *'liberal humanist'*. The chapter concludes by considering whether Leavis had one consistent identity as a critic or more than one. It completes the outline of his life and career that was begun in the first chapter by highlighting four different profiles that emerge from his work between the 1930s and the 1970s (five if we take into account the notion of 'the Leavises').

TRADITION: LEAVIS AND MATTHEW ARNOLD

Leavis was part of a movement in literary study which *seemed,* in the 1920s and 1930s, quite new. The newness was partly a matter of tone – impatience with the amateurishness of earlier critics – and partly a matter of identification with contemporary writers, the writers we now tend to label 'modernist', who were genuinely innovative and challenging. Leavis's thinking is in many ways grounded in his interpretation of the work of two such writers – T. S. Eliot and D. H. Lawrence – figures of such importance to him that I have based a whole chapter of this book on them (see Chapter 4: 'New Bearings'). But it is equally important to note the 'old bearings' that Leavis steered by. He identified himself explicitly with certain cultural traditions which he felt a responsibility to defend – and he wrote a number of essays (based on a Cambridge lecture course and apparently intended for a book which he never completed) identifying the tradition in criticism which he saw himself as belonging to. The key figures in the tradition are Samuel Johnson (see *AK* 197–218); Samuel Taylor Coleridge (*CAP* 41–52); and Matthew Arnold (*CAP* 53–64; also Leavis 1939) – and of these the most important for an understanding of Leavis's thought is Arnold.

MATTHEW ARNOLD (1822–88)

Son of a famous public school headmaster, Arnold first made his name as a mid-Victorian poet (his 'Dover Beach' and 'The Scholar-Gipsy' are still among the best-known English poems of the period). He then moved on to literary and cultural criticism, and to writing on religious topics. Arnold combined his role as a 'man of letters' with a career as a government school inspector; and he is an important figure in the history of education as well as criticism and poetry (though he never dreamed, as is sometimes suggested, of founding 'English' as an academic subject). *Culture and Anarchy* (1869) and 'The Function of Criticism at the Present Time' (1865) are the works of Arnold with which Leavis has the strongest affinities. But critiques of the Arnold–Leavis tradition often focus on a later essay, 'The Study of Poetry' (1880), in which Arnold described poetry as 'criticism of life' and recommended a 'touchstone' method for the evaluation of poetry.

Arnold was important to Leavis in several different ways, to understand which is to understand something about his concept of 'tradition' generally as well as the particular sense in which he can be described as 'Arnoldian'. He had quite different uses for Arnold the poet and Arnold the critic. As a poet, Arnold was for Leavis a good example of what was wrong with English poetry in the Victorian era and its aftermath, the era before T. S. Eliot came along. He features prominently in the first chapter of *New Bearings in English Poetry*, 'Poetry and the Modern World', as the type of the poet who failed to engage with the modern world. As a critic, on the other hand, Arnold articulated an essential insight into the modern world. He was the best model, for Leavis, of the 'central' critic, one who understood that against 'disintegration' could be set the notion of 'a certain ideal centre of correct information, taste and intelligence' (quoted in Leavis 1939: 97); and that against 'worship of machinery' should be set 'culture ... getting to know, on all the matters which most concern us, the best which has been thought and said in the world' (Arnold 1965: 233) Leavis had a different idea from Arnold of what that best was (he thought much more highly than Arnold of provincialism and puritanism, for example), but he had the same idea of its essential role in the world. Indeed, he did not devote much space in his writing to explaining or justifying Arnold's view of culture – it was a fundamental premise that he took over and adapted to twentieth-century conditions. When Leavis writes specifically about Arnold, it is something else he particularly highlights as providing a useful model – not *what* Arnold thought about culture but the *mode of thought* about it which he particularly exemplifies. Arnold proves, Leavis suggests, that 'there is more than one kind of valuable thinking':

[T]here may be an important function for an intelligence that, in its sensitive concern for the concrete, its perception of complexities, and its delicate responsiveness to actualities, is indifferent to theoretic rigour or completeness and does not mind incurring the charge of incapacity for strict thinking. ... We may be left feeling that some other word than 'thinker' would fit Arnold more comfortably, but no concession can be allowed that denies Arnold remarkable distinction of intelligence ... if his virtues are to be properly recognized it is important not to apply wrong criteria.

(Leavis 1939: 94–95)

The idea that there can be a different kind of 'thought' from that which is characterised by 'theoretic rigour' is one we will go on to look at in more detail in the next chapter. It is a key issue for Leavis – and a key issue for all debates about literature, criticism, and whether they matter.

'LIBERAL HUMANIST'

At this stage it is useful to take in another term, more potent than 'Arnoldian', which is often used to describe the kind of 'indifferent-to-theoretic-rigour' thinking which Leavis affirms in Arnold. This term is 'liberal humanism'.

The terms 'liberal' and 'humanist' have a vast range of different usages. Plenty of people have in the past been proud to describe themselves, for various reasons, as either 'liberal' or 'humanist'. When these two terms are combined, however, in the context of contemporary literary and cultural studies, they are not generally meant as a compliment but as a way of stigmatising the approach associated with Arnold, Leavis and others. Critiques of 'liberal humanism' usually go something like this:

- 'Liberal humanism' sets up an idea of 'human nature' as something timeless and unchanging.
- It then makes 'human nature' or 'the human spirit' the ultimate reference point for literary study and eliminates from serious consideration all traces of what is *not* necessarily timeless and unchanging – for example, the material differences between particular groups of humans (rich and poor, men and women, ruler and ruled) at particular moments in history.
- It pretends to be about freedom (the word 'liberal' derives from the Latin word for free) and equality (our shared 'human nature').
- But in practice liberal humanism really only serves the interests of a particular (modern, middle-class, patriarchal, Western) social group and uses the appeal to 'human nature' to obstruct any social or political changes which might threaten those interests.

Leavis was suspicious of anything that looked like an abstract notion of 'timeless' truth – he associated it with the traditional influence of the classics (Latin and Greek) and training in the classics – so although references to 'human nature' can be found in his work, they do not have the kind of programmatic force that the caricature above suggests they should. If it is just a matter of finding positive uses of the words 'liberal' and 'human' in his work, on the other hand, Leavis can certainly be convicted of 'liberal humanism'. At the end of his essay on 'Arnold's Thought', for example, Leavis describes Arnold as standing for 'the vigorous and influential existence of a cultivated and responsible public, repository of *a liberal spirit and a humane tradition*' [my italics]. In an earlier essay, 'Marxism and Cultural Continuity', Leavis comes even closer to a classic statement of the 'liberal humanist' idea in his notion of 'autonomy of the human spirit':

> There *is*, then, a point of view above classes: there can be intellectual, aesthetic and moral activity that is not merely an expression of class origin and economic circumstances; there *is* a 'human culture' to be aimed at that must be achieved by cultivating a certain autonomy of the human spirit.

(*VC* 35)

In practice, academic critiques of 'liberal humanism' (and of course there are other kinds of attack it is subject to) tend to be directed not at the fundamental aspirations associated with 'liberal' and 'humane' but rather at what Tony Davies has called the 'final insufficiency' of liberal humanism (Davies 1997: 47). The problem with liberal humanism, in other words, usually turns out to be that in practice it is just not liberal or humane *enough*. It doesn't manage or want to make all humans free. After its universalising pretensions have been demolished, however, some kind of appeal to human life and potential usually re-emerges, because although to regard all references to the 'human' with suspicion and mistrust may be theoretically sound, it seems to lead to a particularly impoverished view of life: that there can never be any shared understanding of the world between human beings (a position which, by definition, would never be worth arguing because it could never be understood by anyone other than the person arguing it).

In Leavis's way of invoking the 'human' there is a slightly different emphasis from my caricature. As the last passage quoted above suggests, in Leavis's view, agreement on what constitutes shared 'human' reality is something to be 'aimed at' and 'cultivated' rather than just assumed to exist and then imposed. As Michael Bell observes, Leavis 'saw fundamental values precisely as cultural creations and was impressed more by their fragility than their power' (Bell 2000: 407). It could be argued, of course, that there is a rather fine line between, on the one hand, *aiming at* a shared perception of the human world and, on the other, simply arriving at your own view of it and requiring the rest of the world to accept that. Leavis does seem at times to cross this line with his particularly robust and coercive – bullying even – rhetoric. He often implies that what he has said is so obvious, so 'plain', that to disagree is to mark oneself out as not really belonging to the community of intelligent readers he is addressing. But there is another feature of Leavis's rhetoric which, while he did not always follow through its implications, is more integral to his version of liberal humanism. It is articulated most clearly in an essay Leavis wrote much later in his career – but one in which he deliberately returned to the theme of the 'autonomy of the human spirit':

> You cannot point to the poem; it is 'there' only in the re-creative response of individual minds to the black marks on the page. But – a necessary faith – it is something in which minds can meet. The process in which this faith is justified is given fairly enough in an account of the nature of criticism. A judgment is personal or it is nothing; you cannot take over someone else's. The implicit form of a judgment is: This is so, isn't it? The question is an appeal for confirmation that the thing *is* so; implicitly that, though expecting, characteristically, an answer in the form, 'yes, but–' the 'but' standing for qualifications, reserves, corrections. Here we have a diagram of the collaborative-creative process in which the poem comes to be established as something 'out there', of common access in what is in some sense a public world … More, it gives us the nature in general of what I have called the 'third realm' to which all that makes us human belongs.
> (*NSMS* 62; also 94)

In Leavis's 'diagram', shared understanding of a poem (and, ultimately, of the world in which the poem exists) depends on a dialogue which begins with the exchange 'This is so, isn't it? … Yes, but … ' and ends in agreement. The opening formula may have a slightly dated sound to it, and may still have an inbuilt bias towards assent rather than dissent ('expecting … an answer in the form "yes … "'). But if you think about it what Leavis has described is essentially the exchange on which most intellectual work is premised. You might object that it would be more appropriate to open with 'This is what I think – I recognise that you may think otherwise – I would be interested to hear what you do think … ' But in fact it is conventional to academic publishing that these assurances are always implicit. In this book I am telling you what I think (about what Leavis thought) but I am not going to come round to your house later to make sure that you agree with what I think. My job is rather to present what I think in such a way as to convince you that what I think is what everyone who considers my argument will think – to be, as it says in the Series Editor's Preface, 'authoritative'. Every statement in this book (and I'm pretty sure in all the others in the series) is implicitly in the form 'This is so, isn't it?' that Leavis described. In his liberal humanism, similarly, though Leavis sometimes appears authoritarian, he does not aspire to be any more than 'authoritative'.

LEAVIS A, B, C …

I suggested in the first chapter of this book that the answer to the question 'Why Leavis?' is necessarily bound up with questions about what 'criticism' is and why. The same could be said about 'What is Leavis?' To answer 'a critic' is really just to rephrase the question, not answer it. During his career there was much controversy over what kind of critic Leavis was – or rather what kind of criticism he was best at. This was particularly so during the 1950s, the period immediately after Leavis's journal *Scrutiny* had ceased to appear, when a number of younger critics and teachers sought to build on Leavis's work with new journals and related projects of their own. A number of essays appeared as part of this process, paying tribute to Leavis's achievements and often proposing what has been described as 'a distinction between Leavis A, the brilliant literary critic, and Leavis B, the cultural polemicist' (Martin 1996: 13). These attempts generally produced a fierce rebuttal by Leavis. He stubbornly refused to hand over the baton on these terms, insisting that, as Martin puts it, 'the literary critic was, and always had been, the cultural critic' (Martin 1996: 13).

Leavis had his reasons for insisting on this non-division, which will be explored further in Chapter 3 ('Culture'). But one cannot really blame his critics for attempting such preliminary distinctions, since one of the main techniques Leavis himself uses in his literary criticism is to distinguish the (usually small) part of an author's complete work that really matters as great art and account for the less successful work in terms of a conflict between different forces at work in the author – or even different identities. There were definitely two T. S. Eliots for Leavis, for example. We have already noted that there were two Matthew Arnolds. There were even two D. H. Lawrences – the one who wrote *Lady Chatterley's Lover* and the one who wrote the truly 'Laurentian' commentary on it, *A Propos of Lady Chatterley* (see *AK* 240). In the chapter structure for this book I seem to have gone much further than the 'Leavis A and Leavis B' critics by fragmenting my Leavis into six or seven different identities. I have done this because of the different *contexts* in which students are likely to come across references to Leavis. But it does go against the grain of Leavis's published *texts*, in which there is a strong tendency towards integration of all the parts into a whole. Leavis habitually recycled his published work, often quoting, sometimes at length, what he had said elsewhere, and combining essays from different periods in new books, as if to deny the implication that his views had changed or developed over the decades. Some of his views did change, but there is a consistency to his thought which hinders systematic sub-division. It is important, nevertheless, to distinguish different phases in the *external* circumstances in which he worked, and the different audiences he engaged. This is what I propose to do now, beginning at the point where I ended my narrative of Leavis's life in the first chapter. Rather than just dividing into an A and B, then, I would suggest Leavis's career can be crudely divided into *four* main phases:

(1) The first phase covers the period in the early 1930s when Leavis emerged as an exciting new critic of contemporary culture. His first book, *New Bearings in English Poetry*, established him as a critic of contemporary poetry, with a clear idea of why poetry ought to matter to the modern world. With the appearance of *Scrutiny* it became clear that he was not a lone voice but the leading figure in a dynamic group of serious-minded men (and one woman) intent on exposing the shortcomings of contemporary culture, while vigorously fending off challenges from left and right. In the early volumes of *Scrutiny* there is a strong sense of dialogue with other journals; and it is noticeable that during this period Leavis increased the sense of a collaborative enterprise by editing several volumes of essays by other writers, as well as assisting in the writing of *Culture and Environment*, an influential school textbook (many of *Scrutiny*'s readers – and some contributors – were teachers).

(2) After the first few years of *Scrutiny*, Leavis seems to have moved into a second phase of his career with a series of essays mapping out English literary history from Shakespeare and Donne through

to the Victorians. This period, from the mid-1930s to early 1950s, corresponds to the period during which he and his wife took over most of the editorial responsibility for *Scrutiny*, and in which Leavis eventually gained more secure employment as a university teacher of English in Cambridge. His writing during this period is more focused on the question of how English literature should be studied and taught as a university subject; reference to new poets and novelists disappears almost entirely (with one important exception – T. S. Eliot).

(3) A third phase can be seen to begin from the mid-1950s, after the end of *Scrutiny* in 1953 and completion of a series of books culminating in *D. H. Lawrence: Novelist* (1955). Free from the pressure to produce copy for the next *Scrutiny*, Leavis wrote fewer journal articles and made the public lecture and published letter his main platforms (see Collini 1998a). He engaged in a number of public controversies, often over what *Scrutiny* had stood for, and this process culminated in a notorious lecture in 1962 in which he launched a fierce attack on C. P. Snow, the novelist and government adviser on science. This was followed by more public lectures in which he attacked other representatives of what he saw as the educational establishment – and various other targets, some particularly ill-advised.

(4) A brief fourth phase probably should be distinguished towards the end of this 'embattled' phase, though there is considerable overlap. This is the period during which Leavis became more focused on philosophical questions such as the nature of 'thought' and the particular claims of literary criticism as distinct from philosophy or theory. The key work from this period is *The Living Principle* (1975).

'THE LEAVISES'?

It is possible that to some readers the question 'Why Leavis?' addressed in the first chapter will have a different inflection: why am I focusing on *Leavis* when I should be talking about *the Leavises*? To a certain extent this presents itself as an ethical question, as there does seem something strikingly inequitable about the way the academic career and profile of Leavis's wife Q. D. Leavis (1906–81 – 'Mrs Leavis' as she was almost always named, though in fact she had the same right to the title of 'Dr Leavis' as her husband) was apparently eclipsed or annexed by his during their lifetime. When Leavis married Queenie

Dorothy Roth in 1929, she was a brilliant graduate of the early 'Cambridge English' course, about to start her Ph.D. (supervised by I. A. Richards). The outcome of her research was *Fiction and the Reading Public*, a bold and highly opinionated book about popular fiction and culture, which probably did more to energise the early '*Scrutiny* movement' than *New Bearings in English Poetry*. In 1932, when both books appeared, the Leavises were on an equal footing – if anything the scholarship-winning thesis-publishing Q. D. looked like more of a high-flyer than F. R. who had taken eight years to produce one book. Yet by the time of his death in 1978 he had almost twenty more highly influential books to his name while she had none (apart from two in their joint names): and he had held (after some setbacks) a permanent academic position for twenty-six years, and various honorary positions there-after, while she had only had occasional part-time work as a college tutor.

Why did it turn out this way? The Leavises themselves apparently saw it as a case of deliberate 'ostracism' or 'persecution' by an anti-Leavis establishment, but other factors have to be considered, includ-ing the long periods of ill-health that Q. D. Leavis suffered, and the traditional but unequal division of domestic (which included secretar-ial) labour that the Leavises seem to have settled on. However, the blame is apportioned, it is not clear that any wrongs are really put right by considering the two different bodies of work that Q. D. and F. R. Leavis produced as the combined work of one composite critic, 'the Leavises'. The label inevitably diverts attention away from the work to the life of the Leavises as a couple, and foregrounds a very late period in their working lives, when they did actually publish two books in their joint names (fulsomely dedicating the second book, *Dickens the Novelist*, to each other). But this later work is not really collaborative, except in the limited sense of agreeing to keep clear of each other's territory. The really creative period of the Leavises' col-laboration was at the beginning, not the end, of their partnership, when Q. D. Leavis's formidable energy and wide reading, combined with the element of quasi-sociological research in *Fiction and the Reading Public*, clearly galvanised her husband's career as a writer, and decisively re-shaped his attitude to the world. It was he, however, who then became the more effective performer and communicator of that attitude. Q. D. Leavis's writing does often furnish a useful gloss on particular emphases in F. R. Leavis's thought, but she is generally less subtle in the articulation of her position, more intemperate in her engagement with other critics, and more explicitly conservative in her attitude to the past. More justice may be done to her achievements by reading against the grain of her strong association with F. R. Leavis and relating her work more to other contexts – particularly other women writers. Some work of this kind is already under way (see Stewart 2004 and Montefiore and Varney 2008).

SUMMARY

This chapter has been about *introducing* Leavis, reviewing some of the ways in which he describes himself and some of the ways in which you are likely to find him introduced in other accounts.

- Leavis explicitly identified himself with a tradition of critical thinking represented most strongly in the nineteenth century by Matthew Arnold.
- This tradition aims to speak authoritatively but unsystematically (and authoritatively *because* unsystematically) about what ought to be truly valued in contemporary culture and what is over-valued.
- It was not exactly Leavis's term, but this kind of thinking can be described as 'liberal humanist' inasmuch as ultimately it is premised on faith in the possibility of human beings arriving at a shared understanding of the world.
- These emphases are consistent even though in other respects his career can be divided into different phases.

2

LITERARY CRITICISM, THEORY AND PHILOSOPHY

This chapter explores the issue that for some is at the heart of what makes Leavis an important thinker and for others is what disqualifies him from being considered as a critical thinker at all. This is his view that literary criticism – his way of engaging with texts – should be thought of as an intellectual discipline existing in its own right, not subject to theory or philosophy. To make sense of this view, the chapter looks at the two sets of texts which are most often cited in discussions of Leavis and 'theory': first his well-known exchange with René Wellek in 1937; and then a group of later writings clustered around *The Living Principle* (1975).

PERSPECTIVES ON 'THEORY'

Four key terms which will recur throughout this chapter are 'Criticism', 'English', 'Philosophy' and 'Theory'. To the first three of these terms, as we shall see, Leavis attached great significance. By 'English' he meant the academic subject concerned with the study of English literature; by 'criticism' he meant the way of engaging with literature that he believed should be the *raison d'être* of 'English'; and by 'Philosophy' he seems to have meant both the academic subject generally known by that title (in Cambridge it actually went by the official name of 'Moral Sciences') *and* the way of thinking which he attributed to that subject and which he saw as fundamentally different from 'criticism'. It is tempting to complete the matrix by labelling this different way of thinking 'theory', and even refer to Leavis's 'hatred of theory' (Samson 1992: 130). But this would be misleading in relation to Leavis's own discourse, in which 'theory' is a relatively neutral term ('I hope I may have advanced theory' we even find him saying, without irony, in the next section). 'Theory' has become a much more loaded term, in the context of literary studies, *since* the period in which Leavis was writing, and to make sense of his position it is essential to take this into account.

Leavis did not use the term 'theory' to refer to an academic phenomenon which he perceived as a threat to criticism. He used it rather in the basic sense in which it is used in most discourses, to refer to a way of thinking and organising ideas which tends to be systematic, abstract and general, rather than descriptive of particular instances. This sense of 'theory' has not gone away, but another usage has developed alongside and around it, whereby 'theory' (sometimes distinguished as 'Theory' or even 'Theory with a capital T') names what is understood to have been a historical event, a change or series of changes that have overtaken 'English' since the period dominated by Leavis. It is difficult to establish a precise narrative of when, where, or to whom this change occurred: references to 'Theory' tend to be accompanied by conveniently vague gestures towards 'the last few decades' (and I have used an equally vague formula in my last sentence). It cannot really be denied, however, that a transformation of some kind has taken place (every degree curriculum for 'English' shows some signs of it) and that 'Theory' is the label that sticks to this transformation (book titles such as *Beginning Theory, Theory's Empire, Reading After Theory* come to mind). It does not follow that 'Theory' has resulted in the study of literature becoming much more systematic and abstract than it was before – indeed the new emphasis has often been on questioning or subverting systems rather than building them. The least contentious way to summarise the changes associated with 'Theory' is to think of them as essentially *bibliographic*; it is the reading lists, and the way they are organised, that have changed more decisively than anything else. Writing about literature is no longer simply identified as 'criticism' but is classified in terms of a range of different critical approaches or practices, many of which would have seemed to previous generations of English students to have nothing to do with the way they thought about literature. Most importantly, influential thinkers from outside the Anglo-American tradition, such as Barthes (1915–80), Foucault (1920–84), Derrida (1930–2004) and Lacan (1901–81), have come to be regarded as important and authoritative sources for literary studies; as have to a certain extent the thinkers who are important sources for *these* figures, such as the philosophers Hegel (1770–1831), Marx (1818–83), and Heidegger (1889–1976); and the founder of psychoanalysis, Sigmund Freud (1856–1939).

It is important to understand that these bibliographical changes are *not* the context within which Leavis discussed the role of 'theory'. He did not encounter these particular changes, in the sense in which I have outlined them, or apparently even anticipate them. He did have a strong sense that 'criticism' needed to be defended against alternative accounts of how literature should be studied. But these alternatives were not necessarily identical or equivalent to those which today's English student is expected to come to terms with. So it should not be assumed from the start that there is an absolute opposition between Leavis and everything that 'Theory' represents.

CRITICISM AND PHILOSOPHY: THE EXCHANGE WITH WELLEK (1937)

It is interesting to note that early in his career Leavis seems to have been well aware of the way the term 'theory' could be associated with progressive change in literary studies. He was himself identified with 'theory' in this sense. In Ian MacKillop's biography of Leavis, for example, there is an interesting quotation from a review of his lectures that appeared in the late 1920s:

> Dr Leavis's lectures contain a great variety of interesting matter which it is impossible to obtain elsewhere. Moreover it is not uninteresting to see how modern critical theory may be applied to various problems which have been the source of so much discussion in the past …

> (quoted in *IM* 96)

Leavis's profile here is not unlike that of the radical advocate of 'theory' in a contemporary 'English' department. The essential difference is the bibliographical one I have outlined: the (then) modern theorists Leavis was eager to promote, T. S. Eliot and I. A. Richards, were still firmly in the Anglo-American tradition.

Leavis continued to allow himself to be associated with 'theory' when he regained a lecturing post, after an interval of several years, in 1936. The lecture lists show that during his first year (and in fact every year thereafter until his retirement in 1962) he gave a lecture course entitled 'Critics and Critical Theory'. The dualism in this title perhaps suggests a growing sense of a necessary distinction to be made between what critics do and what critical theory does. The opportunity to explore these issues more publicly came when Leavis was approached by René Wellek, a Czech academic with a strong interest in English literary history, with an idea for a set-piece exchange of views in *Scrutiny*, the journal Leavis edited. This exchange, which appeared in three consecutive issues of *Scrutiny* in 1937 under the heading 'Literary Criticism and Philosophy', took the form of (1) a letter from Wellek, directly addressed to Leavis; (2) an essay by Leavis, commenting on Wellek's letter but not directly addressing him; and (3) a short further reply by Wellek (to which Leavis added a comment of his own in a footnote, thus securing the last word). The starting-point for the exchange, and the subject of Wellek's opening letter, was Leavis's fourth book *Revaluation: Tradition and Development in English Poetry* (1936). Wellek had admired much in this book and agreed with many of Leavis's observations, particularly on the eighteenth-century poets. But he had a problem with the way Leavis had presented his argument: 'I could wish that you had stated your assumptions more explicitly and defended them systematically'. Wellek admitted that he shared most of Leavis's assumptions, but 'would have misgivings in pronouncing them without elaborating a specific defence or a theory in their defence'. He then went on to list some of Leavis's key terms: 'Allow me to sketch your ideal of poetry, your "norm" with which you measure every poet: your poetry must be in serious relation to actuality, it must have a firm grasp of the actual, of the object, it must be in relation to life ... '. At the end of a long catalogue, Wellek revealed that all the qualities he had listed were simply 'tags' (i.e., key phrases) taken from different chapters of *Revaluation*. Since Leavis obviously could not argue with his own statement of his position, 'the only question I would ask you is to defend this position more abstractly and to become conscious that large ethical, philosophical and, of course, ultimately, also aesthetic *choices* are involved' (Wellek 1937a: 376).

It is for this direct challenge, and Leavis's robust refusal to do what Wellek challenged him to do (defend his position 'more abstractly'), that the exchange with Wellek has become one of the best-known exchanges in twentieth-century literary criticism. But Wellek only took half a page to issue the challenge. The remaining seven pages of his letter were given over to a more specialised case against *Revaluation*: that Leavis's reading of the Romantic poets Blake, Shelley and Wordsworth was weakened by a 'lack of interest in romantic philosophy' (Wellek 1937a: 378). This part of the correspondence is of less interest, except that Wellek's emphasis on 'philosophy' explains the position Leavis deliberately took up in his reply. Wellek had said that he would have 'misgivings' about dealing in untheorised assumptions. Leavis seized on this confession: 'That, I suggest, is because Dr Wellek is a philosopher; and my reply to him in the first place is that I myself am not a philosopher ... I have pretensions – pretensions to being a literary critic ... ' (*TCP* 211). Wellek had not actually said that he was a philosopher; at this time he was in fact, like Leavis, a lecturer in literature. All he had said was that he thought a critical reading of Romantic poetry should take into account the romantic philosophy, or 'view of the world', articulated in the poetry. But Leavis was briskly dismissive of this attempted combination of interests: '"the romantic view of the world" ... yes, I have heard of it; but what interest can it have for the literary critic?' (*TCP* 216). He insisted that literary criticism and philosophy should be recognised as 'quite distinct and different kinds of discipline' (*TCP* 212).

This gesture of distinguishing literary criticism from other discourses (philosophy here, but elsewhere Marxism, sociology, Christianity, historical scholarship, textual scholarship) is foundational for Leavis and recurs throughout his career. But it is interesting to note that in the exchange with Wellek there seem to be two different arguments justifying the gesture. On the one hand there is a pragmatic argument. Leavis suggests that it would be inappropriate for him to do what Wellek suggests because he has already demonstrated a *better* method for achieving the same outcome. This is best illustrated by the passage below:

> I feel that by my own methods I have attained a relative precision that makes this summarizing [Wellek's catalogue of "tags"] seem intolerably clumsy and inadequate ... by choice, arrangement and analysis of concrete examples I give those phrases (in so far, that is, as I have achieved my purpose) a precision of meaning they couldn't have got in any other way. There is, I hope, a chance that I may in this way have advanced theory, even if I haven't done the theorizing.
>
> (*TCP* 215)

The effectiveness or otherwise of one's critical vocabulary, Leavis implies, does not depend on how one defends it 'abstractly' but on how one combines critical terms with 'concrete examples' from the text. If the terms work at all, in other words, it is only because the text as it were speaks through them. This is a very appealing argument, and not just because of Leavis's rhetorical device of opposing his 'precision' to Wellek's 'clumsy ... summarizing'. Wouldn't we rather read poetry than read a theory about poetry? Leavis suggests that in reading effective criticism of a poem, as opposed to some other kind of writing about it, we are in effect reading the poem itself, but with a more precise perception of it than before. Leavis does not even rule out theory altogether, but sees it as a project worth advancing, provided it does not obstruct criticism. In an earlier paragraph he agrees that 'ideally' some sort of theoretical statement ought to 'complete the work ... but I am sure that the kind of work that I have attempted comes first' (*TCP* 214).

Leavis's pragmatic appeal to 'work', to judgement by results, does seem like an effective rebuke to Wellek, and their exchange of views has often been interpreted in this way. Wellek had conceded at the outset that Leavis had produced 'acute critical observations and brilliant interpretations of texts' (Wellek 1937a: 376). Why should he then 'defend his position more abstractly'? Wellek's answer, in his further reply to Leavis, is that Leavis misrepresents the nature of what the critic does: 'after all' Wellek notes, 'right as you are in insisting on what you call "complete response" as an indispensable preliminary to criticism, it is only a preliminary and the critical problem begins with the translation into language which cannot be other than conceptual, at least to a very high degree'(Wellek 1937b:196). This is where it becomes apparent that the difference between Leavis and Wellek is more than just a matter of the relative efficiency of different methods, since Leavis does not seem to acknowledge that the 'critical problem' is to do with 'translation'. His idea of what the critic does, as set out in the following passage, is more radical in its implications:

> By the critic of poetry I understand the complete reader; the ideal critic is the ideal reader. The reading demanded by poetry is of a different kind from that demanded by philosophy ... Philosophy, we say, is 'abstract' (thus Dr Wellek asks me to defend my position 'more abstractly'), and poetry 'concrete'. Words in poetry invite us, not to 'think about' and judge but to 'feel into' or 'become' –

> to realize a complex experience that is given in the words … The business of the
> literary critic is to attain a peculiar completeness of response and to observe a
> peculiarly strict relevance in developing his response into commentary.
>
> (*TCP* 212–13)

In describing what the critic does here, Leavis emphasises 'reading' rather than writing, and suggests that the words which make up the critic's commentary are 'demanded' by the poem rather than chosen by the critic. The issue of 'translation into language' which Wellek sees as the beginning of the 'critical problem' does not really come into focus. Neither does Leavis seem to acknowledge Wellek's basic premise that criticism involves 'large … *choices*' about which one should 'become conscious'. Leavis describes what the critic does in terms which imply the opposite of consciousness and choice. In poetry we are not invited to 'become conscious' but simply to '"become"'. The syntax of Leavis's sentence actually breaks down after this word is reached, suggesting almost a lapse of consciousness. Become … what? The phrase which is brought in to restart and complete the sentence, 'realize a complex experience that is given in the words', implies we become something we are not; what becomes real to us is something that actually belongs to someone else's consciousness. This process is described in terms of something being 'given', but what it involves seems more involuntary – a process of taking, or perhaps even being taken over.

I am not trying to suggest here that Leavis believed criticism should take the form of some kind of primitive emotional surrender to the words of the text: in his account of what reading should involve, as we shall see in later chapters, the emphasis is often quite the opposite. But it is worth noting here, nevertheless, a certain ambivalence towards the values implied in Wellek's references to consciousness, choice and translation into language. To put it another way, Leavis does not endorse Wellek's idea of the critic as a fully conscious and authoritative speaking subject. An ironic feature of the exchange is that, because Leavis chose not to address Wellek directly but refer to him in the third person, his elaborately courteous 'reply' is regularly punctuated with reminders of Wellek's academic title: 'I must thank Dr Wellek … Dr Wellek knows what it is … If Dr Wellek should still insist … ' One cannot help being reminded that Leavis was also entitled to call himself 'Doctor', by virtue of the award of the degree of Doctor of *Philosophy* – and later in his career was universally known as 'Dr Leavis'. The title is just a matter of academic convention of course (Wellek's title from his Prague university was Doctor of *Philology*) but it could be argued that the idea behind the convention is one of the key ideas on which academic institutions are based: that there is a common conceptual framework within which different kinds of knowledge and inquiry can be evaluated and related to each other – and that this framework is provided by abstract theory or philosophy. Wellek seems to have been invoking this idea when he asked Leavis to defend his position 'more abstractly'. Leavis, despite his formal title, seems ambivalent about the idea that 'philosophy' sums up what a university should be about.

RENÉ WELLEK (1903–95)

Educated in Vienna and Prague, Wellek was working in England as a lecturer in Czech language and literature when he made his contributions to *Scrutiny*. He had previously worked with the Prague Linguistic Circle, and later in the 1930s he moved to America where he became a leading figure in 'Comparative Literature' and in writing the history of literary criticism. His influential *Theory of Literature* (with Austin Warren, 1949) effectively did for American 'New Criticism' what he had offered to do for Leavis in 1937, but he was later critical of certain developments in 'Theory' which he saw as an 'attack on literature'.

LANGUAGE AND THOUGHT: *THE LIVING PRINCIPLE* (1975)

Leavis's fifteenth book, *The Living Principle* (1975), appeared almost forty years after the exchange with Wellek, but its roots can be traced back to the same period. In the early 1930s, Leavis had actually promised his publishers a book on critical method, which may have been what he had in mind when he admitted to Wellek: 'Ideally I ought perhaps … to be able to complete the work with a theoretical statement' (*TCP* 214). The publishers knew this book by the title 'Judgment and Analysis', although Leavis apparently also referred to it by the working title 'Authority and Method' (*IM* 223). Parts of it (close readings of a number of passages of poetry) were published in *Scrutiny* over the next twenty years, but the book as such never materialised – evidence perhaps that Leavis found the task of producing a 'theoretical statement' of his approach more than just a procedural formality as he had implied to Wellek. Instead, the 'Judgment and Analysis' material eventually resurfaced as a chapter in *The Living Principle* (1975), an extreme (but by no means untypical) example of Leavis's readiness to reuse earlier work in new contexts.

The Living Principle is certainly one of Leavis's most remarkable books. It has been described as his '*summa*' (a complete statement of his position – see, for example, Dean 1998: 8) and he himself describes it as a 'comprehensive manifesto' (*LP* 25). It is not his most accessible work, however: Leavis admits that it requires a 'collaborative reader' prepared to work with 'disconcerting oddities of structure, sequence and inclusion' (*LP* 14). The chief oddity is that the book is divided into three starkly contrasting parts, and it is not immediately clear how, if at all, the different parts are related. In the first part, 'Thought, Language and Objectivity', Leavis seems to come closer than anywhere else in his writing to an explicit statement (or at least exploration – the prose style is particularly dense and elliptical) of his fundamental criteria and assumptions. The second part, 'Judgment and Analysis', reprints (with some important additions: *LP* 97–106; 134–44) the essays previously published in *Scrutiny*, which together make up a series of close readings of about thirty different texts. The third and longest part of the book presents a continuous close reading and discussion of just one text, T. S. Eliot's *Four Quartets*, the work on which Leavis had already written numerous essays. So Leavis seems to be bringing three quite different projects to a conclusion within the pages of one book; and yet is clear that he sees them all as belonging to one argument. The key to this argument, and to understanding *The Living Principle* as both *summa* and 'manifesto', is to be found in the book's subtitle: '*English' As a Discipline of Thought*. Leavis is vigorously affirming the discursive distinctiveness and academic credibility of literary criticism – his way of engaging with literary texts. The argument is continuous with the position he set out in the exchange with Wellek (*LP* 32). But the key terms have been refreshed. In 1937 'thought' had been more Wellek's term than Leavis's; it was Wellek, for example, who had wanted to affirm 'the coherence, unity, and subtlety of Wordsworth's thought' (Wellek 1937a: 379) and Leavis who had argued that this was not the business of the literary critic. Now Leavis is concerned to redeem 'thought' from its conventional associations with the abstract or systematic and identify it with literature: 'What we have to get essential recognition for is that major creative writers are concerned with a necessary kind of thought' (*LP* 20).

What kind of thought is this 'necessary' creative kind, though? 'Heuristic' is one key term Leavis uses to define it, meaning thought which is the opposite of 'clear' and 'logical' because it is not translated into language but only comes into existence as language is used: 'you can't, without basic reservations, subscribe to the assumptions implicit in "clear" and "logical" as criteria without cutting yourself off from most important capacities and potentialities of thought which of its nature is essentially heuristic and creative' (*LP* 97). Another term Leavis associates with this kind of 'thought' is 'the unstatable': 'what is inexpressible in terms of logic and clarity, the unstatable, must not be excluded from thought' (*LP* 43). At one level Leavis's defence of 'English as a discipline of thought' in these terms is still essentially pragmatic and empirical, based on an appeal to the experience of the reader. The use of language in a great creative work is 'the fullest use of language' (*LP* 13) and as we attend to this use – give poetry the 'reading demanded by poetry' in Leavis's earlier words – we realise how inadequate most analytical terms and concepts are to such a task. Even supposedly literary categories like 'imagery' risk appearing naïve and reductive when applied to the 'fullest use of language' in Shakespeare. Leavis's main purpose in reprinting thirty or more close readings in the middle chapter of *The Living Principle* is to enforce this point, which is suggested again and again in his reflections on critical method in relation to particular texts. Literary criticism, he implies, is essentially that which does a better job of representing poetry to us, and realising the 'thought' which poetry is, than any systematic or concept-bound theoretical approach.

But this does not seem to be the whole of what Leavis wants to say about 'English as a discipline of thought' in *The Living Principle*. Rather than leave 'the unstatable' as an empty category, the first and last chapters attempt to fill it by articulating what 'thought', in a truly great creative work, must in some sense always be *about*. What we find in 'Thought, Language and Objectivity' is not one definitive answer to this question (we are talking about the 'unstatable' after all) but a series of formulations: some new to Leavis's writing, some familiar from his earlier essays, and some borrowed from other writers. To make his point Leavis relies quite heavily, for example, on a comment made by the artist–poet William Blake about his designs: 'Tho' I call them Mine ... I know that they are not Mine' (*LP* 44; Keynes 1966: 792).

Another key quotation for Leavis at this time, also used as a touch-stone for the 'thought' of the great creative artist, is from D. H. Lawrence's novel *The Rainbow* (1915), where the narrator says of the character Tom Brangwen: 'he knew he did not belong to himself' (*LP* 46; Lawrence 1986: 75). With these two quotations in mind, both about belonging rather than owning, Leavis formulates towards the end of the chapter an equivalent principle: 'All writers of major creative works are driven by the need to achieve a fuller and more penetrating consciousness of that to which we belong' (*LP* 68).

Here it is interesting to note that Leavis has echoed one of the key terms of Wellek's challenge back in 1937: 'I would ask you … to become conscious'. But at the same time he has closed off considera-tion of one of Wellek's other key terms: choice. Major creative works exist to make us conscious not of choice but of that over which we do not have any choice – that to which we already belong. Leavis avoids saying directly what this is (thus again denying Wellek's implication that being conscious should mean being able to translate what one is conscious of into conceptual language). But it appears that what he is gesturing towards is language – or rather what language represents and is made possible by: continuity in creative achievement in human living. The title phrase 'the living principle' is also intended to evoke this: 'by [this] term I mean what the major artist as I have character-ized him strives to realize or to become … the "living principle" itself is an apprehended totality of what, as registered in the language, has been won or established in immemorial human living'. (*LP* 68)

THE CRITIC AS 'ANTI-PHILOSOPHER'

Put this way, the stakes seem much higher than they did in the exchange with Wellek. As Leavis seems to be suggesting in *The Living Principle,* criticism is attuned to what is most valuable in 'immemorial human living', while philosophy, with its insistence on 'logic and clarity', is effectively about the denial of this. That the stakes should be so high perhaps explains the recurrence of the phrase 'anti-philosopher' in Leavis's writings around this time. Leavis never actually wrote an essay called 'The Critic as Anti-Philosopher', but a collection of his essays was published with this title after his death, and he apparently left notes implying he had some such intention (*CAP* x; but see also *IM* 405–6). In one of the essays collected, 'Mutually Necessary' (a defence of *The*

Living Principle), Leavis does indeed state 'I call myself an "anti-philosopher"' and explains that he does this because in his view 'most philosophers' never manage to escape from an 'assumption that value-judgments in literary criticism are to be justified by philosophical analysis' and they inevitably locate such analysis at 'the mathematico-logical end of the spectrum' (*CAP* 197). This attitude explains one of the more provocative features of the argument in the first chapter of *The Living Principle*. In the exchange with Wellek Leavis had found it convenient to label Wellek a 'philosopher' rather than a 'critic', even though Wellek was not a philosopher in any specialised professional sense but rather a literary critic who wanted to discuss literature in terms of philosophical concepts. In *The Living Principle* Leavis more recklessly ventures into enemy territory with his case for '"English" as a discipline of thought', criticising the influence of major figures in philosophy, such as Descartes and Wittgenstein, who represent a different attitude to thought.

RENÉ DESCARTES (1596–1650)

French philosopher particularly associated with the idea that human existence should be identified with the activity of the mind ('I think therefore I am') rather than the body. This separation of mind and body is the 'Cartesian dualism' which Leavis associates with 'logic and clarity' and opposes to creative thought.

LUDWIG WITTGENSTEIN (1889–1951)

Austrian-born philosopher who studied at Cambridge before the First World War, returned in 1929 and taught in Cambridge during the 1930s and 1940s; radically unconventional in both life and work; often acknowledged as one of the most important figures in twentieth-century philosophy. A striking feature of Wittgenstein's career is its division into two distinct phases. The first phase, which culminated in *Tractatus Logico-Philosophicus* (1921–22), does to a certain extent lend itself to Leavis's caricature of philosophy as 'mathematico-logical'. But Leavis's brief friendship with Wittgenstein actually dates from the period (1929–30) when the philosopher was moving into the second phase in his thought, which is much less reductive in its approach to different uses of language.

MICHAEL POLANYI (1891–1976)

Hungarian-born research scientist, who moved to England in 1933 to become Professor of Chemistry at the University of Manchester. He later published a number of books on politics and the philosophy of science. The most influential of these was *Personal Knowledge* (1958) which argued that intellectual enquiry always included an element of 'tacit knowledge' and faith in a natural order.

Any reader with an interest in philosophy is likely to want to challenge Leavis's caricature of philosophy as inevitably 'logico-mathematical', but it is important to note that the particular approach to philosophy which was dominant in Cambridge during the early part of Leavis's career does fit the caricature better than some other approaches (see Cullen 1993: 196–7). It is also important to note that part of Leavis's case against philosophy is that assumptions about the primacy of logic and clarity as criteria for 'thought' are so deeply embedded in modern culture that it is much harder to shake them off than one would think. For this, Leavis blames the French philosopher Descartes, the 'ghost' whose influence since the seventeenth century has tended to 'disable' intelligent thought (*LP* 35). Modern philosophy as represented by Wittgenstein and by Bertrand Russell (1872–1970) provides no help in counteracting this influence and so the business of 'exorcism' (*LP* 35) falls to English. Leavis sees one promising development in modern philosophy, however – the work of Michael Polanyi, the philosopher of science, whose insistence on the element of 'tacit knowledge' in any kind of intellectual enquiry Leavis takes as an 'extra-literary charter' (*LP* 39) for his position. One of the more scandalous features of *The Living Principle* was Leavis's repeated insistence that students studying 'English' would benefit significantly from reading essays by Michael Polanyi, but would not learn anything useful from attending seminars on the linguistic philosophy of Wittgenstein.

Leavis's reflections on Descartes and Polanyi are perhaps not likely to be taken seriously as contributions to *philosophical* debate. It is probably more helpful to think of what Leavis makes of philosophy in *The Living Principle* as a *narrative* in which Descartes, Wittgenstein, Polanyi and others appear as essentially mythical figures – not unlike the mythic figures in the longer poems of William Blake. References to Blake recur throughout the chapter; Polanyi's thought, for example, is described as an 'essential vindication of Blake' (*LP* 53).

Responding to philosophy with narrative is also the technique of another key essay Leavis wrote around this time, 'Memories of Wittgenstein' (1973; reprinted in *CAP*), which describes his brief friendship with the philosopher after he came to Cambridge in 1929. This essay has always been of great interest to admirers of Leavis because it is the only exercise in extended autobiography (as opposed to occasional anecdote) he ever published. Besides providing some fascinating glimpses of the (almost entirely male) social world of academic Cambridge at the end of the 1920s, the essay presents a series of *tableaux* effectively dramatising Leavis's attitude towards philosophy in the 1970s. In each anecdote Wittgenstein behaves in an overbearing or eccentric manner, and Leavis responds patiently but firmly: 'you had, on occasion at any rate, to be firm and final with him' (*CAP* 130). 'Memories of how I put Wittgenstein in his place' is what the essay is really about. A key episode is the one in which Leavis first encounters Wittgenstein and rebukes him for his rudeness to a student. Wittgenstein seems immediately to recognise strength of character in Leavis and says 'We must know one another' but Leavis replies: 'I don't see the necessity' (*CAP* 132). The implied point is not that English and Philosophy should not know each other at all (it has been pointed out that Wittgenstein's words can actually be interpreted as meaning 'surely we already know one another?' (Day 1996: 185)). What Leavis represents himself as resisting, rather, is the idea that philosophy can dictate terms to literary criticism, or become the kind of grounding discipline for literary criticism implied by Wellek. Leavis's 'I don't see the necessity' anticipates what he later states more explicitly as his 'opposing conviction':

> he [Wittgenstein] couldn't in any case imagine that literary criticism might matter intellectually. Even at that time I had an opposing conviction: it was, as it *is*, that the fullest use of language is to be found in creative literature, and that a great creative work is a work of original exploratory thought.

> (*CAP* 143)

This is another statement of the argument for 'English as a discipline of thought' which Leavis presents in *The Living Principle*. But Wittgenstein in 'Memories of Wittgenstein' is presented in a more positive light than 'Philosophy' generally is in Leavis's 'Anti-Philosopher' writings.

Wittgenstein actually has a dual role in Leavis's memoir. Although he stands for the claims of 'Philosophy' which have to be opposed and put in their place by 'English', he is also assigned the role of the individual artist whose genius can only be properly recognised by 'English'. Wittgenstein was 'a centre of life, sentience and human responsibility' and 'a complete human being, subtle, self-critical and un-self-exalting' (*CAP* 132 and 135). These terms are very similar to those Leavis usually reserves for D. H. Lawrence – and indeed, as often happens in Leavis's writings, Lawrence is cited at one point as a kind of touchstone for how Wittgenstein should be judged (*CAP* 135). What matters most about Wittgenstein, Leavis's memoir implies, is something to do with 'human being' which is too important to be left to philosophers and is best understood by the literary artist and literary critic.

LEAVIS AND 'THEORY'

One of the anecdotes in 'Memories of Wittgenstein' which has been most often commented on (Hawkes 1992: 68–71; Stewart 2003) is the one with which Leavis concludes the memoir. Wittgenstein asks Leavis to 'explain' a poem he admires; Leavis starts to do so but Wittgenstein keeps interrupting ('Oh! I understand that ... But what does this mean?') and eventually takes over the explanation with the words 'Give me the book' (*CAP* 145). Leavis interprets this anecdote in personal terms, suggesting that it shows 'an intellectual incompatibility and perhaps something like an antipathy of temperament' between himself and Wittgenstein. Bearing in mind its context in Leavis's later work, it could also be interpreted in terms of anxiety about the contest between 'criticism' and 'philosophy': although kept in his place throughout most of the narrative, Wittgenstein unexpectedly usurps Leavis's authority at the close. The story could even be interpreted as prefiguring the subjection of 'criticism' to 'Theory' in the historical sense – or not even *pre*figuring but just figuring it, since in many accounts of 'Theory' the changes were well under way by the early 1970s. 'Give me the book!' is in many ways exactly what 'Theory', with its emphasis on re-reading, new accents, new perspectives and so on, has demanded of traditional literary criticism. But reading Leavis's anecdote in this last way highlights the historical irony of Leavis's 'anti-philosopher' stance at this time, for in fact the changes associated with 'Theory' did not really come from the direction Leavis was facing.

'Theory', like Leavis, has generally been anti-Cartesian; it could even be said to have been anti-philosophical in many of its manifestations, inasmuch as it challenges some of the fundamental premises of Western philosophy. It is not usually associated with Wittgenstein's thinking about language. Indeed, in relation to 'Theory', Wittgenstein does not really figure as a key 'critical thinker' at all (as the current list of titles in this book series indicates). 'Theory' is more often described as originating in ideas about language developed by the Swiss linguist Ferdinand de Saussure (Structuralism), and then undergoing numerous transformations and diversifications (for which the best collective term is Post-Structuralism) as it picked up ideas from many other strands in European thought and history. None of these developments register at all in Leavis's later work, even though historically they overlap.

What then can we make of Leavis's thinking in the context of 'Theory'? A number of different ways of answering this question have emerged in the decades since Leavis's death. The answer that has been heard most loudly and often is: nothing. We can make nothing (or nothing good) of Leavis and 'theory' because Leavis seems to stand for the closing off of new possibilities of critical thought and 'theory' stands for openness to them; if we want to do 'theory', therefore, we must set aside Leavis. This approach is implicit in the structure of many textbooks which provide an introduction to 'theory' and which often *start* with a chapter on the shortcomings of 'liberal humanism', 'moral criticism', or 'Anglo-American criticism' in which Leavis is a prominent figure (see, for example, Barry 1995: 16; Newton 1992: 8; Selden 1989: 17). But the best example of a highly developed, authoritative and uncompromising version of this position is the work on Leavis of the British Marxist critic Francis Mulhern. Mulhern is certainly no evangelist for all aspects of 'theory', and he has registered great respect for Leavis's 'peerless militancy' (Mulhern 1979: 331). Nevertheless he sees Leavis's approach to criticism as 'obscurantist' (i.e., opposed to enlightened reform) and 'fetishistic' (i.e., investing literature and criticism with a special status even though they are made of the same basic stuff – English – as other uses of the language). Mulhern recognises that for Leavis 'the literary … exposes the inadequacies of rational inquiry' but he insists that to subject 'rational inquiry' to another discourse in this way 'undermines our only sustainable claim to professional existence' (Mulhern 1995: 82). True critical thinking (or what Mulhern calls 'critical reason') should not look like what Leavis does.

A different way of approaching the question of Leavis and theory has been developed by Michael Bell, who has suggested that Leavis's anti-Cartesian approach to language, thought and 'being' can be aligned with some of the continental thinking which has fed into 'theory' – specifically, Leavis can be seen as 'the English analogue of Nietzsche and Heidegger' (Bell 2000: 400; see also Bell 1988: 35–56). In some respects, then, what 'theory' is about is also what Leavis is about. This helps to explain why, despite Mulhern's strictures and despite the advent of 'theory', Bell is able to claim that Leavis's approach to reading has not gone away but 'some version of his stance effectively underlies, in suffused and implicit ways, much of the everyday reading and study of literature; even where this is overtly denied'(Bell: 1988: 2). In a rather different style, but with similar aims, Gary Day has suggested that Leavis can be seen to have at least 'affinities' with a range of different modern theorists (Day 1996).

A more radical but still carefully reasoned approach to the question of Leavis's relation to 'theory' is that represented by Barry Cullen (Cullen 1993; see also Joyce 2005) who reaffirms Leavis's humanism as an alternative to 'theory'. Cullen is appreciative of Michael Bell's work but also impatient with the idea that Leavis needs a philosophical pedigree in order to be taken seriously. Leavis is never going to provide us with 'a congenial mode of intellectual procedure' because his approach requires 'an attitude in some respects approaching that of religious belief and conviction rather than that of philosophical enquiry' (Cullen 1993: 204).

How we respond to these different approaches to Leavis depends on how we think about ourselves as readers and critics; how we think about 'literature'; and above all how we think about the context in which we engage with it. 'Theory' does not provide definitive answers to these questions; it just provides a longer menu of possible answers. Mulhern's reference to 'professional existence' is a reminder that these questions are in any case rarely just about theoretical possibility but also involve questions of *responsibility* – and the social or institutional frameworks (for example, a profession or a university) from which one derives one's responsibilities. Cullen's reference to 'belief and conviction' also invokes the idea of responsibility – but in this case responsibility towards what one personally believes, rather than the institution within which one believes. This raises awkward questions about whether a discourse based on 'belief and conviction' can ever have a comfortable relationship with an institution like a university or an academic profession. But that is part of what makes Leavis an interesting figure: in his career we see a lifelong experiment in *un*comfortable relationships.

SUMMARY

Towards the end of his career Leavis refreshed some of his terms and became more reckless in his comments on the shortcomings of 'philosophy', but the defence of criticism he outlined in *The Living Principle* (1975) is basically the same as the one he set out in his exchange with Wellek (1937). The underlying principles of this defence are:

- It is not in works of philosophy but in great literature that we encounter the most important kind of 'thought'.
- This kind of 'thought' is creative rather than empirical or analytical; it transcends the limitations of 'logic and clarity' and draws to the fullest possible extent on the resources of 'immemorial human living' available in a particular language.
- 'Criticism' means 'realising' this kind of thought (or realising its absence in works which do not come up to the standard of the greatest literature).
- 'Criticism' in this sense is not a systematic process; its preoccupation should be with the 'reading demanded' by the text rather than the critical terms chosen by the critic.
- 'Criticism' should be the main business of 'English' as an academic discipline; it should not be regarded as depending for its authority on translation into abstract philosophical concepts.

In one way or another, these principles can be seen to inform Leavis's treatment of all the topics to be covered in the rest of this book.

3

CULTURE

In the volume of the recent *Cambridge History of Literary Criticism* in which Leavis appears, critics are introduced under three different headings. T. S. Eliot, not surprisingly, appears under the heading of 'Modernists'. I. A. Richards and William Empson are treated as 'New Critics'. Leavis, however, appears, with the American critic Lionel Trilling (1905–75), under a third heading: 'The Critic and the Institutions of Culture' (see Bell 2000). This classification makes a lot of sense. It partly reflects the fact that in Leavis's writing analysis of literature rarely goes on for long without some embittered reference to the 'institutions of culture' framing the critical work: the academic world, the literary world, and so on. But it also reflects the fact that for Leavis the study of literature is inseparable from the study of what literature is a part of – for which 'context' is one word but 'culture' is another. This chapter focuses on the way Leavis thought about 'culture' by looking at three main texts which are particularly associated with this topic in his work: the early pamphlet, 'Mass Civilisation and Minority Culture' (1930); the school textbook *Culture and Environment* (1933); and the text of his controversial 'Richmond Lecture' *Two Cultures? The Significance of C. P. Snow* (1962). But it starts by briefly considering the relation of Leavis, who is usually associated with the academic subject 'English', to the history of the academic subject 'Cultural Studies'.

LEAVIS AND 'CULTURAL STUDIES'

'Literary' is one of those words which Leavis uses opportunistically, sometimes with positive connotations and sometimes with negative (as in his contemptuous references to 'the literary world'). In the following passage we can see him attempting to distinguish the positive from the negative:

> For to insist that literary criticism is, or should be, a specific discipline of intelligence is not to suggest that a serious interest in literature can confine itself to the kind of intensive local analysis associated with 'practical criticism' – the scrutiny of the 'words on the page' in their minute relations, their effects of imagery, and so on: a real literary interest is an interest in man, society and civilization, and its boundaries cannot be drawn; the adjective is not a circumscribing one.
>
> (*TCP* 200)

Leavis does not want the adjective 'literary' to have the effect of limiting or drawing boundaries around what the critic does, but in practice that has often been its effect. Another adjective has often seemed more appropriate for the kind of work Leavis describes – 'cultural' – and with this has come in due course the name of a new discourse, 'cultural studies'.

One has to describe 'cultural studies' as a discourse rather than an academic subject, because it is not always visible as a named subject in the curriculum of particular academic institutions (as indeed 'literary studies' is not). In most it has a flourishing existence, however, and is sometimes regarded as having subsumed (or as threatening to subsume) literary studies. Perhaps because of these institutional ambiguities, 'Cultural Studies' has evolved a strong sense of its own history – or rather histories, as there are different narratives for different parts of the world. In the history of British Cultural Studies, two important founding figures are Richard Hoggart and Raymond Williams; and the discourse is often thought of as coming into existence towards the end of the 1950s, when Hoggart published *The Uses of Literacy* (1957) and Williams published *Culture and Society* (1958). Another key date is the establishment of a Centre for Contemporary Cultural Studies, presided over by Hoggart, at Birmingham in 1964.

According to this narrative, Leavis does not belong to the history of Cultural Studies so much as its *pre*history. He is recognised as an important influence on both Williams and Hoggart, both of whom are often described as having started out as 'Left-Leavisites'. Williams used the title 'Culture and Environment' for the early form of cultural studies he developed in his adult education classes – a reference to Leavis and Thompson's *Culture and Environment* (1933), which was widely used as a textbook in adult education as well as secondary schools (see McIlroy 1993: 30–1). As Francis Mulhern has shown, however, Leavis is representative of an older European tradition of writing about 'culture' – known as *kulturkritik* (see Mulhern 2000) or sometimes 'culturalism' (Milner 1994) – and 'Cultural Studies' evolved from attempts to challenge the basic principles of this earlier tradition. Leavis's main contribution to 'Cultural Studies', then, is probably the negative one of giving 'Cultural Studies' something to define itself against. In relation to the quotation above, such a critique might well start by questioning the assumptions behind the gendered reference to '*man*, society and civilisation' – and perhaps also detect a tone of imperialist heroism in the phrase 'its boundaries cannot be drawn ... ' But criticism of Leavis's model of culture generally starts with the distinction between 'culture' and 'civilisation' which was the keynote of one of his first important publications.

'MASS CIVILISATION AND MINORITY CULTURE' (1930)

The title seems to say it all in 'Mass Civilisation and Minority Culture', a pamphlet published by the Minority Press, a venture set up by one of Leavis's former students. Not only does it spell out the basic antithesis, it is also clearly designed to echo Matthew Arnold's equally explicit title *Culture and Anarchy* – but with the terms reversed to add the implication that (as Leavis says in his opening sentence) '[f]or Matthew Arnold it was in some ways less difficult'. Arnold could assert the primacy of 'culture' without self-consciousness; now, Leavis implies, the anarchy of 'mass civilisation' is dominant and no values can be taken for granted. It therefore becomes necessary for Leavis to define what he means by 'culture' rather than simply refer back to Arnold's definition. He does this in the following passage, which you may remember from the first chapter of this book:

> The minority capable not only of appreciating Dante, Shakespeare, Donne, Baudelaire, Hardy (to take major instances) but of recognising their latest successors constitute the consciousness of the race (or of a branch of it) at a

given time. For such capacity does not belong merely to an isolated aesthetic realm; it implies responsiveness to theory as well as to art, to science and philosophy in so far as these may affect the sense of the human situation and of the nature of life. Upon this minority depends our power of profiting by the finest human experience of the past; they keep alive the subtlest and most perishable parts of tradition. Upon them depend the implicit standards that order the finer living of an age, the sense that this is worth more than that, this rather than that is the direction in which to go, that the centre is here rather than there. In their keeping, to use a metaphor that is metonymy also and will bear a good deal of pondering, is the language, the changing idiom, upon which fine living depends, and without which distinction of spirit is thwarted and incoherent. By 'culture' I mean the use of such a language.

(*FC* 14–15)

It is not surprising that this passage is so often quoted in critical summaries of Leavis as it seems densely packed with what Rene Wellek would later call 'norms' ('finer living', 'distinction of spirit', 'thwarted and incoherent', 'the nature of life'). One statement that seems to require some further explanation is the penultimate one that 'in their [the minority's] keeping ... is the language', which Leavis says is both a metaphor and a metonymy. This means that culture is in some way *like* a language (likeness is the basis of the figure of speech known as metaphor) but language is also associated with culture by being part of what it is (association or belonging is the basis of the figure of speech known as metonymy). Appreciating 'the nature of life' may be *like* knowing a language, but such knowledge also *requires* the full use of language and can never be crudely or abstractly summarised (this – as we saw in the last chapter – was an idea Leavis would later reformulate as 'the living principle').

There are various things one might query or object to in Leavis's account. But the big theoretical problem with his model is the one that has been characterised by the Canadian critic Pamela McCallum as 'the polarisation of society and consciousness' (McCallum 1983). McCallum and others have probed the issue of the *connection* between mass society and the minority who represent 'consciousness'. Her argument is that Leavis was unable properly to explain the relationship implicit in his formula 'mass civilisation *and* minority culture', because his cultural theory, inherited from Arnold, entailed an impasse between 'the conception of a harmonious enclave of culture disjunct from society and an equal insistence on the efficacy of that sphere in society' (McCallum 1983: 4). How can minority culture influence the rest of society, in other words, if it is essentially different in kind from everything else which constitutes society? And if it is not essentially different, why is culture always right and society always wrong? Is it possible to imagine that society might one day influence culture for the better, rather than assuming that the influence must always work the other way? From Leavis's point of view, no purpose would be served by exploring these questions. Who would want to equate Shakespeare (or his 'latest successors') with the latest Book Society choice or other examples of popular leisure criticised in the early volumes of *Scrutiny*? From a 'Cultural Studies' point of view, however, it is important to conceptualise such an equation, because it is a way of trying to establish that the values which the minority hold are ultimately social in origin. They are not just recognised by society but are formed by society, and as such they are not absolute but can change as society changes; once this is recognised, the role of culture in *preventing* society from changing can also be addressed. One thing Leavis and 'Cultural Studies' do agree on is that society *ought* to change; what they disagree on is how change can be generated. Leavis believes in the Arnoldian idea of 'culture' bringing about change indirectly by making its presence felt; Arnold claimed that culture 'told silently' (Arnold 1965: 106). 'Cultural Studies', on the other hand, starts by seeing this notion of 'culture' as part of the problem rather than the solution.

'THE MACHINE' VERSUS THE 'ORGANIC COMMUNITY': *CULTURE AND ENVIRONMENT* (1933)

I have just said that Leavis believed society should change. But if you look again at the famous paragraph quoted above from 'Mass Civilisation and Minority Culture', you might wonder where I am getting this from. The paragraph seems to describe an ideal order prevailing at any 'given time', in which tradition is 'perishable' but essentially in the right safe hands (the 'keeping' of the minority). It is part of the effectiveness of Leavis's rhetoric (and perhaps also symptomatic of the 'polarisation' problem we have just looked at) that he contrives to evoke a sense of classical order *and* at the same time tell a story of apocalyptic collapse. It is never quite clear in the end which is history, though at this particular point in 'Mass Civilisation and Minority Culture' Leavis seems at pains to make this clear: 'the modern phase of history is unprecedented'. To support this belief 'it is enough to point to the machine. The machine, in the first place, has brought about change in habit and the circumstances of life at a rate for which we have no parallel' (*FC* 16).

'The machine' takes many different forms in Leavis's account – new technology is the most obvious one (Leavis refers in old-fashioned idiom to 'the automobile' and 'the films') but there is also the use of applied psychology in advertising; mass circulation of newspapers; any process of 'levelling down' and 'standardisation'. A similar range of phenomena is surveyed via some study exercises in *Culture and Environment*. Everything Leavis highlights does belong to what he calls 'the modern phase of history' (i.e., the twentieth century) but his reference to 'the machine' also echoes Arnold's repeated references to 'machinery' and 'over-valuing machinery' in *Culture and Anarchy*, which in turn echo similar references in earlier writers. So there is a sense in which 'the machine' is as much a timeless mythical enemy as a particular mid-twentieth-century problem. What Leavis ultimately means by 'the machine' is close to what Arnold means by it: any systematic, external, abstract approach to social problems which does not take account of individual human circumstances or needs or of traditional wisdom.

The opposite of a machine-driven society is what Leavis called an 'organic community' – that is, a society in which people relate to each other more intuitively, creatively and holistically, and with more of a sense of natural order and continuity between past and present. The idea of such an alternative is implicit in Leavis's emphasis on the machine. But if he had simply posited 'organic community' as an ideal to be worked towards, or as something long lost in the past, there would have been nothing particularly distinctive about Leavis's analysis. *Culture and Environment* makes the much more dramatic and explicit claim that the organic community really did exist, historically and within living memory, and has only just been 'lost'. 'Its destruction (in the West) is the most important fact of recent history – it is very recent indeed. How did this momentous change – this vast and terrifying disintegration – take place in so short a time?' (*CE* 87). As evidence for the existence of the organic community, and the process by which it was lost, one main source is quoted from extensively: the works of George Sturt (1863–1927). Sturt was an English writer who combined running a traditional family business, a wheel-making shop in Farnham,

Surrey, with writing about country life. In his two best-known books, *Change in the Village* (published under the pseudonym George Bourne) and *The Wheelwright's Shop*, Sturt describes in detail the highly skilled traditional craftsmanship of his employees and the 'art of living' which characterised their community life – both of which he observed being gradually eroded by the impact of new technologies and a more systematic organisation of work into an activity separate from the rest of life. Several chapters of *Culture and Environment* are given over almost entirely to long quotations from and elaboration of Sturt's books, with particular emphasis being placed on the social interaction which was part of the old village life, the fulfilment the tradesmen found in their work ('Besides their hands their brains, imagination, conscience, sense of beauty and fitness – their personalities – were engaged and satisfied' (*CE* 75)), and the part played by tradition ('the experience of ages') in the learning of their trade.

Many critics have pointed out that Sturt's testimony, if examined closely, does not do exactly what Leavis and Thompson want it to do in *Culture and Environment*. Anne Samson notes that in Sturt's account one problematic group of workers – the sawyers – subvert the 'organic' idyll and reintroduce an element of class conflict into his history (Samson 1992: 54). Gary Day suggests that the figure of the wheel itself (associated with *revolution*) generates ironies which also undermine the ideal of a linear social order (Day 1996: 73). Other critics have been openly scornful of *Culture and Environment*'s claim that an 'organic community' ever existed: 'this aspect of Leavis's work appears to me so transparently erroneous that I do not intend to let it detain me any longer' (Lawford 1976: 9). But the classic and more measured critique was formulated by Raymond Williams in his analysis of Leavis in *Culture and Society*. Williams notes that references to the organic community are always more nostalgic than historical: 'If there is one thing certain about "the organic community", it is that it has always gone' (Williams 1961: 252). But he then rather surprisingly confirms, from his own experience of village life in the 1920s and 1930s, that some of the features of community life and work which Sturt describes did exist. He argues, however, that *Culture and Environment*'s way of representing this never describes the whole social experience: 'it is foolish and dangerous to exclude from the so called organic society the penury, the petty tyranny, the disease and mortality, the ignorance and frustrated intelligence which were also among its ingredients' (Williams

1961: 253). In other words, the 'organic community' did exist, but it was never the completely *adequate* community – the community that 'engaged and satisfied' – that more nostalgic accounts require it to have been; Leavis and Thompson were mistaking part for whole.

Leavis later described *Culture and Environment* as an 'opuscule' (minor work; see *LC* 58) and resisted requests from his publisher to update the material in it. The book probably should not bulk so large in discussions of Leavis's thought as it often does. Its approach to history via Sturt served to make it a stimulating textbook for a while, but in the longer term – and in the context of Leavis's whole career – the references to the 'organic community' make more sense if they are interpreted figuratively. What Leavis was really interested in was not country life (Sturt was hardly mentioned again after *Culture and Environment*) but the problem of how to maintain social and intellectual community in the modern world. A term that recurs frequently in his later writing, equivalent in some respects to 'organic community', is 'educated public' – meaning a public which could be relied on to validate and disseminate the judgements of the minority referred to in 'Mass Civilisation and Minority Culture'. The significance of the wheelwright in this context is that he symbolises a particular approach to thought, and the authority of the shared values and understanding on which continuity depends. 'Truly, it was a liberal education to work under Cook's [the wheelwright's] guidance' Sturt says in one of *Culture and Environment*'s many quotations; he had 'a knowledge as valid as any artist's. *He knew, not by theory, but more delicately* ... ' (*CE* 84; my italics).

THE 'TWO CULTURES' CONTROVERSY

The term 'culture' features particularly prominently again in Leavis's writing in his Richmond Lecture, 'Two Cultures? The Significance of C. P. Snow', given at Downing College, Cambridge, in February 1962 (the occasion was an annual formal lecture, which Leavis was invited to give, named after a former head of the college, Admiral Richmond). He followed this up a few years later with a lecture on the same topic, 'Luddites? or There is Only One Culture', and four more lectures on related themes – all of which were published together as *Nor Shall My Sword: Essays on Pluralism, Compassion and Social Hope* in 1972. The lectures clearly belong together, and it is easiest to access them in *Nor Shall My Sword*. But the Richmond Lecture was first published, accompanied by cartoon images of Leavis and Snow, a week after it was given, in *The Spectator*, the weekly London-based periodical. It is worth looking up the March 1962 issues of *The Spectator*, to get a sense of the strong reaction the lecture caused: the following week *The Spectator* printed five pages of letters on it, and more over the next three weeks, and Leavis's lecture was also widely commented on and debated in other publications. The lecture was from Leavis's point of view a brilliant publicity coup – except in the sense that by generating so much publicity it actually gave the 'two cultures' thesis he was attacking a much longer life in public debate than it might otherwise have had.

The subject of Leavis's lecture was C. P. Snow (soon after Lord Snow), and the primary reason for the controversy it generated was what Leavis sarcastically called 'my notorious exhibition of bad manners at poor Lord Snow's expense' (*NSMS* 90). The lecture was devastatingly critical of Snow, and included several statements that *The Spectator*'s solicitor advised were potentially libellous, including that Snow was 'portentously ignorant' and 'intellectually as undistinguished as it is possible to be'. But Leavis shrugged off all criticisms of his 'bad manners', dismissing them as 'willed refusal to see and understand' and comparing his own role to that of the child in the Hans Andersen story 'The Emperor's New Clothes' (*NSMS* 70). He reacted bitterly to criticism from Lionel Trilling who suggested that some sort of breach of professional ethics had been involved: Trilling spoke of 'a bad tone, an impermissible tone' that 'manifestly intends to wound' (Trilling 1966: 150). Leavis saw the lecture in quite the opposite way, as an exercise of professional responsibility with 'no personal animus in it' (*NSMS* 68). Snow had managed to get a way of thinking about culture widely accepted which was false and damaging; 'drastic finality' was necessary to expose him.

But what had Snow said that was so 'portentously' wrong? Snow had started his famous lecture, 'The Two Cultures and the Scientific Revolution' (1959; see Collini 1998b), by identifying two cultures which were influential in British public life: the scientists and the 'literary intellectuals'. Because he was an accredited member of both cultures he was well qualified to introduce both and to mediate between them, but on the whole they did not understand each other and this was bad for the country as a whole. It is sometimes assumed that this is the whole of the 'two cultures' thesis: scientists and artists do not know enough about each other. But as with most oppositions one term was privileged – Snow's argument was really that the 'literary intellectuals' were conservative, selfish, and indifferent to human suffering in their resistance to technological innovation and its benefits. Another misconception is that Leavis's reply was an attack on scientists. It was rather an attack on Snow's public authority and his way of adjudicating between science and literature. Snow did not understand what a 'culture' was – his caricature of 'literary intellectuals' did not represent in any way the real significance of great literature and the nature of its critique of technology. As the cultural historian Stefan Collini has noted, the debate 'involved the clash of fundamentally opposed convictions of how to think about human well-being' (Collini 1998b: xxviii). All Leavis's ideas about culture, about 'man, society and civilization', converge in his critique of Snow. Snow was *'portentously* ignorant' – that is, a portent, a sign of something wrong – and what was wrong was the lack of an effective educated public. If such a public existed, Snow's view of culture would never have been taken seriously and Leavis would not have needed to give his lecture. But at the same time the lecture provided the stimulus to develop several new ways of expressing positively what Snow had not understood and had dismissed as 'literary culture'. Culture was the achievement of shared understanding and values: 'a prior human achievement of collaborative creation ... the creation of the human world, including language' (*NSMS* 61).

C. P. (CHARLES PERCY) SNOW (1905–80)

At the time of Leavis's lecture Sir Charles Snow (he was knighted in 1957 but as a novelist was still identified as C. P. Snow) had a high public profile as a successful novelist and scientific expert. He had been a research scientist in the 1930s and (like Leavis) a Fellow of a Cambridge College; during and after the war he worked as a government adviser. His novels dealt with intrigues in the academic, scientific and political worlds (the 'corridors of power') that he had moved in. Leavis's attack probably dented Snow's reputation as a novelist, but did not damage his establishment career. His modernising emphasis on the need for society to embrace the 'scientific revolution' chimed well with the rhetoric of 'technological revolution' which helped to bring Labour to power in 1964. In that year he was made a member of the House of Lords and between 1964 and 1966 he served as a junior minister in a newly created Ministry of Technology in the Labour government.

'TECHNOLOGICO-BENTHAMITE'

Leavis's intervention against Snow – and later other establishment figures he labelled 'Snow-men' – also led to his coining of the term 'technologico-Benthamite' to characterise the attitude he opposed. This term has become a useful shorthand for the main target of Leavis's cultural criticism and is even occasionally used now without reference to Leavis at all. He actually did not start using it in his writing until the mid-1960s. One of its first appearances was as the title of a later lecture at Cambridge, 'Why *Four Quartets* Matters in a Technologico-Benthamite Age' (*ELTU* 111). By 'Technologico-Benthamite age' Leavis meant an age in which the benefits of technological and economic progress were over-valued and the dominant way of thinking about human well-being was in material and statistical terms – as in the suggestion, often associated with Bentham, that 'pushpin is as good as poetry' if it gives an equal amount of pleasure. Concerns about technology ('the machine') and its effects on society had been present in Leavis's discourse from the beginning, but 'technology' was a particular buzz-word of the mid-1960s. Hostile references to the philosopher Jeremy Bentham (1748–1832) and to Utilitarianism, the philosophical system with which he is strongly identified, had also been recurrent in Leavis's work since the mid-1930s (see particularly *VC* 151; and Leavis 1950).

SUMMARY

Leavis's ideas about 'culture' owe much to the Arnoldian tradition with which he identified. His early writings, particularly 'Mass Civilisation and Minority Culture' (1930) and *Culture and Environment* (1933), made an important contribution to thinking about 'culture' in the twentieth century, even though 'Cultural Studies' since the 1960s has tended to define itself by its attempts to move away from the 'minority' emphasis in Leavis's model. Leavis's ideas can be summarised as follows:

- 'Culture' means 'the human world' – the shared understanding of human well-being, need and potential accumulated over the ages and represented above all in the shared language of a community.
- 'Culture' is not inert but must be kept alive – like a culture in a laboratory – to be passed on from one generation to the next.

- In the past, 'culture' was kept alive by the 'organic' nature of community life.
- In the twentieth century, the modern world has developed in ways not sanctioned by 'culture' but determined by the uncontrolled use of new technologies and a 'Benthamite' attitude to value.
- In such a world, responsibility for keeping 'culture' alive lies with the minority or 'educated public' who are still capable of recognising and defending it.
- Such a public should be capable of recognising and exposing travesties such as C. P. Snow's 'two cultures' thesis, which proposed that 'culture' was just a reactionary preoccupation of modern 'literary' intellectuals and that scientists were more progressive in their approach to human well-being.

4

NEW BEARINGS

At the very beginning of his career, as we saw in the last chapter, Leavis identified 'culture' with 'the minority capable not only of appreciating Dante, Shakespeare, Donne, Baudelaire, Hardy (to take major instances) but of *recognising their latest successors*' (*FC* 15; my italics). Shakespeare remained central, but the other authors mentioned as 'major instances' here did not play a great part in Leavis's later work. The task of 'recognising their latest successors', on the other hand, was foundational, and his first book, *New Bearings in English Poetry: A Study of the Contemporary Situation* (1932), was devoted to this task. It established Leavis as an authoritative critic of contemporary poetry, but did so by installing another critic as the ultimate authority: T. S. Eliot. The new bearings were those which Eliot had made possible: *New Bearings* was 'a tribute' to Eliot, who had made possible a re-reading of past and present, and Leavis's whole career as a teacher and critic was in a sense founded on insights that he got from Eliot. But it was also founded on the insight that Eliot was not enough. There had to be another 'successor' to the tradition – D. H. Lawrence: 'our time, in literature, may fairly be called the age of D. H. Lawrence and T. S. Eliot'(*DHLN* 303). This chapter looks at why these two figures were so significant for Leavis – and what each signified; and it concludes by looking briefly at Leavis's comparative neglect of other writers who constituted 'the contemporary situation'.

T. S. (THOMAS STEARNS) ELIOT (1888–1965)

No account of twentieth-century 'modernism' in English literature would seem complete without reference to T. S. Eliot's poem *The Waste Land* (1922). Eliot was born in the American mid-west, into a prosperous family with powerful religious and academic connections, and was highly educated, studying at Harvard, Paris and Oxford. He moved to England in 1915 and stayed for the rest of his life. His complete poetry only fills one volume but he also wrote numerous critical essays and even before *The Waste Land* his first collection of essays, *The Sacred Wood* (1920), had made a strong impact, particularly in Cambridge. 1922 was also significant as the year in which he launched the quarterly journal, *The Criterion*, which ran under his editorship until 1939, and served as both a model and a target for *Scrutiny*.

D. H. (DAVID HERBERT) LAWRENCE (1885–1930)

Lawrence was born and brought up in a large mining village in Nottinghamshire, England. He escaped the limited career options of most young men in the area by gaining a scholarship to secondary school, and later training as a teacher at the university college in Nottingham. He soon gave up teaching and spent the rest of his life writing and travelling – hardly returning to England after the war. Several of his novels, notably *The Rainbow*, *Women in Love* and *Lady Chatterley's Lover*, were initially banned for their sexual content – an uncensored version of *Lady Chatterley's Lover* did not become available in England until 1960, after the publisher Allen Lane won a famous legal case. Lawrence was a prolific writer, not just of novels but of short stories, poems, travel books and unconventional critical and philosophical essays. Leavis and Lawrence never met, but it was highly significant for Leavis that Lawrence had once visited Cambridge and been repelled by the lifestyle of the privileged intellectuals he met there (see *TCP* 255–60). This encouraged Leavis to think of himself and *Scrutiny* as representing an alternative, more Lawrence-inspired, Cambridge.

'ELIOT'S HEAD AND LAWRENCE'S TAIL'

The Garland *Annotated Bibliography* of the Leavises has an Appendix itemising all F. R. Leavis's writings on Eliot and Lawrence. The list runs to over sixty separate items (twenty-four on Eliot and thirty-nine on Lawrence; Baker *et al.* 1989: 447). What is particularly striking about the list is that it covers (for both authors) almost the whole of Leavis's career as a writer. He published his first essay on Eliot in 1929 and his first on Lawrence in 1930; his last book, published in 1976, was on Lawrence; and the last-but-one, published in 1975, contained a 100-page essay on Eliot. It is not unusual, of course, for an academic to devote most of his career to research on one or two particular authors and to produce a large body of work in the process. But this is not really the kind of work Leavis was doing on Eliot and Lawrence: his essays were almost entirely about why and how Eliot and Lawrence were important. Nor does the Garland list really convey the extent of his preoccupation with them: the listed essays are the tip of an iceberg which extends under a great deal of writing on other topics as well. References to Eliot or Lawrence (or both) turn up in almost every book, often as a touchstone or standard for a particular judgement of another author. A quotation from D. H. Lawrence pops up, for example, in the middle of Leavis's 'Revaluation' of Wordsworth; another appears in 'Memories of Wittgenstein'; another in an essay on Shakespearean tragedy. Phrases from Eliot are just as frequent. The two figures are far from interchangeable, however. Being so different, there was a perpetual tension between them in Leavis's thinking, as registered in the comment I quoted in my first chapter: 'Eliot's head and Lawrence's tail do not fit together at all' ('Ille Ego' 1933). From the mid-1930s onwards Leavis tended to recoil from Eliot towards Lawrence, but this in many ways made the tension more productively dynamic – not so much an iceberg, more a nuclear reaction.

A good example of the way this worked is in Leavis's use of the phrase 'the common pursuit of true judgment', a description of criticism from Eliot's essay 'The Function of Criticism' (1921). The phrase encapsulated Leavis's idea of criticism as both purposeful (directed towards 'true judgment' even if never likely to reach it) and collaborative ('common'). In 1951 he acknowledged how useful he found it, but turned this into an opportunity to distance himself from Eliot and identify himself more with Lawrence:

> For criticism is essentially a collaborative business; a critic cannot be unaware that he is engaged in 'the common pursuit of true judgment'. This formulation is Mr Eliot's and I own I find it a useful one. But does that make me a follower

of Mr Eliot? (The suggestion that I *am* one must, I think, be as surprising to him as it is to me.) To call me a follower of Dr Johnson and Matthew Arnold and D. H. Lawrence, critics with whom I find myself much more in sympathy, would be less misleading.

(Leavis 1951: 502)

Leavis used the phrase 'the common pursuit' again the following year as the title for his new collection of essays – and due to this it is now associated with Leavis much more than with Eliot. But the first essay in the collection, 'Mr Eliot and Milton', is severely critical of Eliot and accuses him in effect of having bowed to establishment pressure to change his views about Milton. Naming the book after Eliot's description of criticism thus becomes less of a tribute, more of a pointed rebuke. One factor in this pattern may simply have been that Lawrence was dead, incapable of adding anything to his life's work, while Eliot remained alive and all too capable of doing and saying things that undermined Leavis's reading of his work. Eliot occasionally corresponded with Leavis; and Leavis often told the story of how in the 1940s Eliot visited him at his home in Cambridge, an event which Leavis interpreted as Eliot trying to confess and be absolved of some unspecified wrong he had done to him. It is interesting to speculate how the Eliot–Lawrence dynamic in Leavis's thought might have been different if Lawrence had not died abroad in 1930 but through some improbable chain of circumstances returned to England, become an 'establishment' figure, and eventually come knocking on Leavis's door in the 1950s to ask him to appear as a witness in the 'Lady Chatterley trial'.

LEAVIS AND ELIOT

Leavis's view of Eliot's importance can be crudely summed up as follows: Eliot wrote some important criticism in the 1920s and some important poetry in the 1930s. Leavis's map of Eliot thus looks rather different from the usual one, in which the most prominent landmarks tend to be (for literary studies) his poem *The Waste Land* (1922) and (for cultural studies) the essays on culture which he produced in the 1930s and 1940s. For Leavis *The Waste Land* was impressive, but essentially just an exemplification of the case Eliot was making in his criticism around the same time. The later criticism avoided the key cultural issues but the series of poems that began with *Ash Wednesday*

(1930) and concluded with *Four Quartets* (1935–42) were 'heroic' in their exploration of these issues.

There isn't really one essay by Leavis, out of the twenty-four listed in the Garland *Annotated Bibliography*, that one can point to as the definitive statement of his attitude to Eliot. Several useful summaries already exist which track in more detail the apparent changes from one essay to the next (see particularly Black 1975; Bergonzi 1984; Kearney 1989). I am going to take a different approach in this section and focus on three more critical concepts or phrases which, like 'the common pursuit', were thrown out fairly casually by Eliot in his early essays but taken up very seriously by Leavis and built into the foundations of his critical practice. By 'seriously' I do not mean that Leavis took up these terms in any deferential, talismanic way. He recognised that they were, in a sense he particularly respected, opportunistic: 'Eliot wrote in a particular situation at a particular time and under journalistic conditions – he took the opportunity; and took it in a way that after all produced a classical and decisive piece of criticism' (*ELTU* 91). The point is that Leavis regarded the insights on which the terms were based as essentially right – and as remaining right even after Eliot himself had apparently come to see things differently. Their authority derived not from Eliot himself but from their applicability beyond Eliot's own use of them. The three terms are: 'dissociation of sensibility', tradition, and 'altered expression'.

Eliot used the phrase '*dissociation of sensibility*' in an essay on 'The Metaphysical Poets' (1921: see Eliot 1953: 117) to express his sense of how English poetry in the eighteenth and nineteenth centuries differed from the poetry of the early seventeenth century. The difference was to do with the synthesis of thought and feeling in language in the earlier period. The earlier poets (and the dramatists of Shakespeare's era who came before them) had possessed a 'mechanism of sensibility which could devour any kind of experience'; they did not treat some experiences as intrinsically more poetical than others. At some point in the century, however, 'a dissociation of sensibility set in, from which we have never recovered', after which poets generally lacked this responsiveness. Eliot's description of the 'dissociation of sensibility' as a historical event ('something which ... happened to the mind of England') has been heavily criticised over the years; in this respect and others it finds its counterpart in Leavis's account of the 'loss of the organic community'. Leavis was aware of the criticism, and was circumspect about repeating

Eliot's exact term (*LA* 38; *ELTU* 96). But he subscribed fully – more so than Eliot – to the idea that the seventeenth century was the key moment of transition in English cultural history when something of great value was lost. It was Eliot's insight into this that he was particularly paying tribute to in *New Bearings*: 'It is not for nothing that Mr Eliot's criticism has been directed mainly upon the seventeenth century. One might say that the effect of his criticism and his poetry together has been to establish the seventeenth century in its due place in the English tradition' (*NBEP* 198).

'Tradition and the Individual Talent' (first published in two parts in 1919; see Eliot 1953: 21–30), which sets out Eliot's idea of *tradition*, is probably the best known of all his essays. Leavis's attitude to it was complex. He eventually came to deplore the suggestion in the second part of the essay that poetry should be an 'escape from emotion' and an 'escape from personality'. But he remained convinced of the principle Eliot set out in the first part, that 'no poet, no artist, has his complete meaning alone' but becomes significant through a dynamic relationship with 'a living whole of all the poetry that has ever been written'. He extended Eliot's principle to cover the novel as well, and got round the unworkable notion of 'all the poetry that has ever been written' by withholding the status of true 'poetry' from all but a few texts. Most importantly, Eliot's essay furnished Leavis with an idea of tradition which allowed for what he later called 'a new emphasis on the *social* nature of artistic achievement' (*TCP* 183). Contrary to what is generally believed about Leavis, it is actually one of the most deeply engrained characteristics of his literary criticism to analyse a text in relation to a context – to assess the individual achievement as part of the life of a community rather than just as 'words on the page'. The reason he is not usually credited with an interest in context is because Eliot's essay allowed him to conceptualise context – the 'social' – in terms different from those which critics usually have in mind when they insist on context. He did not conceptualise it in political terms (that is, in terms of the distribution of economic power between different social groups at a particular moment in history) but more in terms of what Eliot called an 'ideal order'.

The idea of '*altered expression*' derives from a passage in Eliot's introduction to an edition of Samuel Johnson's poems (1930). The relevant passage is worth quoting in full, as it was of such significance to Leavis:

> Sensibility alters from generation to generation in everybody, whether we will or
> no: but expression is only altered by a man of genius ... [second-rate poets] have
> not the sensitiveness and consciousness to perceive that they feel differently
> from the preceding generation, and therefore must use words differently.
>
> (Eliot 1953: 164)

The phrase 'altered expression' (the equivalent of 'new bearings') recurs often in Leavis's criticism, right to the very end – it is even there in the notes which he left unpublished at his death (*VC* 299). It provided the necessary complement to the idea of tradition that Leavis developed from 'Tradition and the Individual Talent', by providing a more active role for the individual artist than that which had been outlined in the unsatisfactory second part of that essay. Then the implication had been that the lived experience of the individual artist was irrelevant to the artistic process. Now a more heroic model was available, which Leavis was able to apply to Eliot himself. 'Altered expression' explained what Eliot had achieved in *The Waste Land*. But it also provided Leavis with a way of reading English literary history from Shakespeare to Eliot. All his subsequent canon-making (the work we will look at in the next chapter) would be based on the idea that tradition was kept alive and viable by the great individuals who were able to change it.

By 1930, then, from Leavis's point of view, Eliot's work was essentially done. He had provided the conceptual framework for an assessment of contemporary poetry and for a reading of 'tradition' in English literature. Leavis's 'tribute' to Eliot was to apply this framework, first in *New Bearings* and then in *Revaluation* and *The Great Tradition*. What Eliot had not done so usefully, before 1930, was contribute significantly to the project of cultural criticism – the campaign to raise awareness of the effects of 'the machine' – that Leavis was simultaneously engaged in, via *Scrutiny* and *Culture and Environment*, in the 1930s. *The Waste Land* is often thought of as a devastating critique of modern civilisation (the clue is in the title) but Leavis does not seem to have been particularly interested in Eliot's most famous poem in these terms. In 1930, however, Eliot published *Ash Wednesday*, a short sequence of poems with a pronounced religious theme, and Leavis seems to have found much more of strategic value in these poems, and those that followed them, than in the earlier work. Their importance to him seems to be encapsulated in the lecture title 'Why *Four Quartets* matters in a technologico-Benthamite age' which he used for a lecture in 1967. But the best place to examine Leavis's reading of these poems in more detail is probably the essay 'T. S. Eliot's Later Poetry' which is reprinted in his wartime book *Education and the University* (1943). Here Leavis puts Eliot's poetry forward as a model for the kind of disciplined resistance to modernity that education should be about:

> To have gone seriously into the poetry is to have had a quickening insight into the nature of thought and language; a discipline of intelligence and sensibility calculated to promote, if any could, real vitality and precision of thought; an education intellectual, emotional and moral.

> (*EU* 104)

Eliot's later poems are often taken as expressing his Christian faith and allegiance to the Church of England, but Leavis insisted on reading them against this grain. Christian doctrine was just a 'frame' for the poems but what they were really about – what the reader would have 'gone seriously into' if he read them as Leavis read them – was the essential kind of 'thought' that explores the nature of reality without the help (in practice more like obstruction) of any theological or philosophical system. The poetry seemed to signal Eliot's acceptance of Christian doctrine but in fact it was 'essentially a work of radical analysis and revision ... heroic in its *refusal* to accept' (*EU* 103; my italics). Leavis reserved his highest praise for Eliot to the end of the essay, where he likened him to D. H. Lawrence in that he had 'stood for the spirit in these brutal and discouraging years' (*EU* 104).

LEAVIS AND LAWRENCE

It was high praise indeed for Leavis to compare Eliot to Lawrence, for by this time Leavis was well on the way to regarding Lawrence as 'our last great writer' and 'the great writer of our own phase of civilization' (*DHLN* 9). More often, when Leavis made this kind of statement, he took it as an opportunity to remind his readers of how Eliot had failed to recognise Lawrence's greatness. During the 1930s and 1940s Eliot had published several critical assessments of Lawrence, suggesting that Lawrence was an undisciplined genius who had not fulfilled his potential because he was 'ignorant' and 'uneducated'. Reaction against these and similar disparaging comments seems to have played an important part in Leavis's growing admiration for Lawrence and disaffection from Eliot. Indeed he seems to have taken some of Eliot's disparaging comments on Lawrence as personal comments directed at himself. In 1931, for example, Eliot tried to imagine what an academic version of Lawrence might have been like: 'had he become a don at Cambridge his ignorance might have had frightful consequences for himself and for the world, "rotten and rotting others"' (Eliot 1931: 771). Leavis repeated this phrase a number of times, claiming that in the early 1930s his own reputation was exactly that which Eliot imagined for Lawrence. He *was* in effect that 'don at Cambridge' – 'widely supposed ... to share the honour of the intention [ie of "rotting others"] with Lawrence' (*DHLN* 311). Leavis also strongly resented Eliot's suggestion that, because of Lawrence's working-class provincial background, he was somehow cut off from the most important cultural traditions in English life. Although Leavis was the son of a Cambridge businessman rather than a Nottinghamshire miner, he felt he had more in common with Lawrence, culturally, than he had with Eliot: 'It is when I come to these things in Mr Eliot that I find myself saying: "*I* am a fellow-countryman of D. H. Lawrence"' (*DHLN* 306).

The British critic Sean Matthews has noted that, in identifying so strongly with Lawrence's emergence from a lower-class provincial background, Leavis was anticipating a significant trend in post-war English literary studies. Several generations of teachers and writers from similar backgrounds (often caricatured as 'scholarship boys') would see Lawrence as articulating their own experience; and see Eliot's condescension as typical of the attitude they came up against as they tried to gain access to the educational establishment. Matthews labels the 1950s 'the Lawrence decade' for this reason (Matthews 1997: 53) but also notes that, while Leavis helped at first to shape this phenomenon, it ultimately developed into something he did not like any more than he liked Eliot's condescension. In 1960, Lawrence's last novel, *Lady Chatterley's Lover*, was the subject of a famous court case in which numerous eminent professional critics, writers and teachers testified that, despite the explicit sex scenes and repeated use of the word 'fuck', the novel was not obscene and should not be banned from sale. Richard Hoggart and Raymond Williams appeared for the defence; T. S. Eliot also attended but was not called to testify (Matthews 1997: 46). Leavis was asked to appear but refused, explaining afterwards that he did not want to be associated with what he called the 'new orthodoxy' on Lawrence that tended to make sexual liberation the keynote of Lawrence's work (*AK* 235). The Lawrence who had written *Lady Chatterley's Lover* was 'not the normal Lawrence' and had actually gone *against* the values of his 'finely civilized upbringing in a Victorian working-class home' to write the sex scenes.

It had all looked rather different back in 1930, the year of Lawrence's death and of Leavis's first exploratory essay on his work. Lawrence was then still a minor cult figure rather than the twentieth-century icon he later became. By his own account Leavis first read a story by Lawrence in 1914; and from 1919 onwards read his books as they came out (*DHLN* 9). But his early essays show that it took him a while to decide just how high a valuation Lawrence deserved – and for what exactly he deserved it. In 1930, *Lady Chatterley's Lover* is the one novel by Lawrence which Leavis is prepared to be positive about, whereas *Women in Love*, the novel which he later came to regard as Lawrence's greatest work, is described as hard to get through. *Lady Chatterley's Lover* appealed at this moment because several passages in it strongly supported the case about 'the machine' and its effects which Leavis was making in 'Mass Civilisation and Minority Culture' and *Culture and Environment*. At one point, for example, the narrator observes: 'The industrial England blots out the agricultural England ... The new England blots out the old England. And the continuity is not organic, but mechanical'. This and several other key passages from the novel (including the description of Connie's drive through Tevershall which begins 'The car ploughed uphill ... ') were quoted approvingly in *Culture and Environment* (*CE* 94). But Leavis still hesitated over the novel as a whole and even wondered whether E. M. Forster's *A Passage to India* might not be more wholesome, and less dangerous, in its insights into modern civilisation.

The problem for Leavis at this early stage was that he recognised Lawrence as a 'genius', comparable to Blake, but he was uncomfortable with what he called the 'teaching' (*FC* 144) or 'conclusions' which pervaded Lawrence's writings – meaning the passages of abstract sermonising about spontaneity, impulse, primitive consciousness and so on, which occasionally interrupt the narrative in the novels and also fill a series of shorter Lawrence books such as *Psychoanalysis and the Unconscious* and *Fantasia of the Unconscious*. Leavis finds this discourse (which he notes Lawrence himself called 'pseudo-philosophy' (*FC* 119)) monotonous and 'mechanical' and perhaps even dangerous: 'of *Lady Chatterley's Lover* we ask: If we accepted this, and all it implies, without reserves, what should we be surrendering?' (*FC* 132). What we find in Leavis's numerous subsequent writings on Lawrence is a gradual working-out of this problem, until in *D. H. Lawrence: Novelist* (1955) it is more or less resolved. The following passage from an early *Scrutiny* essay is representative of this process in Leavis's thought about Lawrence:

> If we find him great, the supreme importance of his books is perhaps that they assure us that he existed … Here was a man with the clairvoyance and honesty of genius whose whole living was an assertion of what the modern world has lost. It is plain from his books that he was not able to maintain steady confident possession of what he sought – wholeness in spontaneity; a human naturalness, inevitable, and more than humanly sanctioned; a sense, religious in potency, of life in continuity of communication with the deepest springs, giving fulfilment in living, 'meaning' and a responsive relation with the cosmos. But it is equally plain that he didn't merely seek.

> (*FC* 147)

Here we have Leavis's wish-list for the modern world; a set of alternative values, inspired by Lawrence's writings, which can perhaps be summed up in the term 'human naturalness … more than humanly sanctioned'. But the books are only a substitute for the 'whole living' we glimpse in them. This early emphasis on Lawrence's life is in keeping with the nature of the critical debate about him in the 1930s, which as Sean Matthews notes was dominated by biographical accounts rather than focused on the novels. Leavis was particularly impressed by Lawrence's letters (1932), which he reviewed in *Scrutiny*. A decisively new phase in his engagement with Lawrence began in the late 1940s, however, when he began a series of essays on Lawrence's fiction which were eventually published together as *D. H. Lawrence: Novelist* (1955). The emphasis in the title is supposed to fall on *novelist* – this is 'where the centre lies' and the answer to the questions '*What*, above all, is Lawrence? As what shall we primarily think of him?' (*DHLN* 17). But in giving his answer Leavis is prepared to be (as always) drastically selective. Of the eleven novels Lawrence published during his lifetime, Leavis recognises only two as of major importance – *The Rainbow* and *Women in Love*, and *Women in Love* as pre-eminent. Besides these, Lawrence's best work, for Leavis, is represented by shorter narratives – particularly the long stories (sometimes referred to as *nouvelles*) *The Captain's Doll* and *St Mawr* (which Leavis regards as a kind of equivalent of *The Waste Land*, but with more 'creative and technical originality' (*DHLN* 225)).

All Lawrence's writings, Leavis frequently admits, show his genius in using language – he 'writes out of the full living language with a flexibility and creative freedom for which I can think of no parallel in modern times' (*DHLN* 226). What distinguishes *Women in Love* is a matter of two other qualities for which key terms are 'organized' (*DHLN* 151) and 'diagnostic' (*DHLN* 155). *Women in Love* is pre-eminent for Leavis because no scene or detail is redundant or discordant – everything plays its part in the overall organisation of effect; and the effect is a powerful 'diagnostic' critique of English civilisation. This is focused above all in the character of Gerald Crich, the son of the local mine owner and thus particularly associated with industrialisation. In Gerald's destructive relationships with Gudrun Brangwen and others we see, Leavis claims, 'the malady of the individual psyche as the essential process of industrial civilization' (*DHLN* 158); and making us see this is what Lawrence as novelist does best. But the negative criticism of Gerald implies a positive standard or an alternative – the 'whole living' that Leavis glimpsed behind 'the books' – and Leavis is more ambiguous on the form that this takes in the novels. To a certain extent the alternative is supposed to be represented by the other couple in the novel, Ursula Brangwen and Rupert Birkin. But Leavis admits he is not sure that they are convincing in this role ('Birkin and Ursula, as a norm ... leave us wondering' (*DHLN* 28)); and even if they are successful in their relationship with each other, the death of Gerald leaves them detached from any sustaining community, faced with 'the question of the kind of success possible in marriage, and in life, for a pair that have cut themselves finally adrift' (*DHLN* 181).

A similar point can be made about Leavis's reading of *The Rainbow*, the novel which tells the story of Ursula and the previous generations of the Brangwen family, and to which *Women in Love* is a kind of sequel. Near the beginning of the first chapter of *The Rainbow*, there is a highly sensuous description of the farming life of the Brangwen family, which Leavis admired, often quoted, and used in his teaching. One expects to find Leavis praising the intimacy of the people with each other and with nature as an evocation of 'human naturalness' or even the 'organic community' – and he clearly did value it for this. But in his analysis of *The Rainbow* his emphasis is on how this 'life of "blood-intimacy" is, in the novel, a necessary and potent presence as something to be transcended. The novel has for theme the urgency, and the difficult struggle, of the higher human possibilities to realize themselves'

(*DHLN* 99). This 'difficult struggle' is embraced by Ursula, who, like Lawrence (and Leavis) goes onto higher education and a different kind of life. The organic community is what has to be left behind. What Leavis produces from his reading of the novels, then, is an answer to his concern about whether Lawrence was 'dangerously a theorist' (*DHLN* 156). He was not, because he did not substitute his 'teaching' for 'fidelity to the concrete': like Eliot he was 'heroic in his refusal to accept'. The novels actually occupy the space between 'steady confident possession' of what Lawrence sought and merely seek[ing].

LEAVIS AND 'MODERNISM'

To attack 'modernist' poetry, Leavis suggested in 1932, is 'absurd', because 'there is no "modernist" poetry, but only two or three modern poets' (*FC* 48). *New Bearings in English Poetry* is Leavis's fuller account of who these two or three poets are. Eliot is obviously the definitive modern poet. W. B. Yeats is also acknowledged to have achieved, in a few poems at least, an authentically modern style (a style, in other words, which has shaken off the influence of the Victorian poetic tradition and demonstrates instead 'the equivalent of certain seventeenth-century qualities' (*NB* 44)). But Yeats was an exception and 'no serious poet could propose to begin again where Mr Yeats began' (*NB* 50). The other contemporary poet given major consideration in *New Bearings* is Ezra Pound, who in Leavis's view had produced one great poem, *Hugh Selwyn Mauberley*, but had so far failed to do anything worthwhile in his ongoing project, the *Cantos*. The difference is a matter of 'a pressure of experience, an impulsion from deep within … ' (*NB* 138) that energises *Mauberley*, whereas 'the *Cantos* appear to be little more than a game' (*NB* 155). Leavis also describes *The Waste Land* in terms of an 'urgency pressing from below' (*NB* 155) and these references to *pressure* 'below' and 'within' are indicative of Leavis's attitude to modernism more generally and explain why he favoured Eliot over Pound, and Lawrence over Virginia Woolf and James Joyce, who would usually figure prominently in any account of modernism but have a fairly low profile in Leavis's reading of 'the contemporary situation'. Leavis admired Joyce's *Ulysses* and used at least one passage from it in his teaching; in the 1920s he was even briefly in trouble with the authorities for proposing to lecture on the novel while it was still officially banned (because of its sexual content) in the UK (*LC* 97; *IM* 88). The passage from *Ulysses* which Leavis particularly admired was the description of a walk on the beach from the third chapter ('Proteus'). Here was prose 'of a Shakespearean concreteness; the rich complexity it offers to analysis derives from the intensely imagined experience realized in the words' (*FC* 208). By contrast Joyce's *Work in Progress* (the work published in occasional parts during the 1920s and 1930s which eventually became *Finnegans Wake* in 1939) lacked any 'impulsion from the inner life capable of maintaining a high pressure' (*FC* 211). Instead of realising an *experience* in words, 'the interest in words and their possibilities comes first' (*FC* 209). Leavis devoted even less attention to Virginia Woolf, but when he did briefly review her work he judged it by similar criteria. Of all her novels he considered *To the Lighthouse* 'the only good one' because the 'substance ... was provided directly by life' – meaning in this case Woolf's own childhood (Leavis 1942: 297). Leavis was suspicious of those aspects of modernism by which it is most often characterised: formal experimentation, 'interest in words and their possibilities'. Where technical innovation could be seen as a way of channelling 'pressure ... from within' – as in Eliot and above all Lawrence – he welcomed it. But where he sensed a gap opening up between words and experience he was dismissive, unwilling to indulge the 'game'. In this respect Leavis's interests are quite markedly different from those of some more recent interpretations of modernism, which have attached great importance to the element of linguistic 'play', particularly in Joyce.

SUMMARY

For Leavis, the most important role of the critic was to ensure that 'culture' as a living tradition was recognised and vindicated – and the most important part of that role was to recognise and work with the important new writers who represented the 'growing tip' (Leavis 1976: 151) of the living tradition.

For Leavis there were two such writers in the twentieth century – T. S. Eliot and D. H. Lawrence. Eliot's contribution to tradition was:

- As a critic to draw attention to the potential of the English language as it was used by poets in the seventeenth century, providing a basic template for the application of this insight in Leavis's criticism.

- As a poet to demonstrate how such potential could be realised again in a way that engaged more effectively with the modern world than Romantic and Victorian poetry had been able to; Eliot's poetry '*matters* in a technologico-Benthamite age'.

Eliot had limitations, however, which also had to be recognised and contested, and it was symptomatic of these that he did not recognise the achievement of the greater writer, D. H. Lawrence. Lawrence's contribution to tradition was:

- In all his writing to show the potential of the English language to articulate the kind of critical but creative thought about life that constitutes 'culture'.
- In his best novels and stories, to articulate a 'religious' insight into life in the modern world without making a religion or theoretical system of that insight.

Recognition of Eliot and Lawrence entailed recognising that other writers often acclaimed as important (for example, Joyce, Woolf, Auden) did not represent the 'growing tip'.

5

GREAT TRADITIONS

T. S. Eliot and D. H. Lawrence deserve their own chapter, in a book on Leavis as thinker, because Leavis seems to have had them so constantly in mind. But if Leavis had *only* written about Eliot and Lawrence, it is unlikely he would be remembered today as one of the most important or talked-about critics of the twentieth century. A much greater part in the building of his public profile was played by his writings on a range of pre-1900 poets and novelists. Applying the values he derived from Eliot and Lawrence, Leavis produced a working outline of English (and to a lesser extent American) literary history between 1600 and 1900. Study of the period 1600–1900 traditionally made up much of the curriculum in 'English' courses (post-1900 claims a much bigger share now but that is a relatively recent trend) so this aspect of Leavis's work had a professional relevance, and engaged a particular professional audience of students and teachers, in a way which is less true of his later writings. This chapter starts with an overview of Leavis's writings on pre-1900 literature; it then looks more closely at the text which is most representative of Leavis's approach in this context, *The Great Tradition* (1948); and finally it explains what Leavis made of two of the most canonical authors in English literature, Dickens and Shakespeare.

MAPPING THE 'WILDERNESS OF BOOKS'

Most of the work I am thinking of was produced by Leavis during the *Scrutiny* period (1932–53), and was first published either in *Scrutiny* or, occasionally, in American journals such as *Kenyon Review* and *Sewanee Review*. Much of it then made its way into two key books, *Revaluation: Tradition and Development in English Poetry* (1936) and *The Great Tradition: George Eliot, Henry James, Joseph Conrad* (1948). Both books were, in a sense, filling in the 'back stories' of Eliot and Lawrence. *Revaluation* surveyed English poetry from Jonson to Keats, and Leavis claimed it had always been planned as a kind of companion to the Eliot-inspired *New Bearings in English Poetry*, to 'complete the account of the present of English poetry with the correlated account of the past' (*RV* 1). When he came to put *The Great Tradition* together, Leavis had yet to write his major book on Lawrence, but it was clearly in development: 'Is there no name later than Conrad's to be included in the great tradition? There is, I am convinced, one: D. H. Lawrence ... the great genius of our time' (*GT* 23). Lawrence actually speaks first in *The Great Tradition*, before any of the specified authors, in a quotation which appears as the epigraph to the book.

As the above outline confirms, there was a shift in Leavis's interest during the *Scrutiny* period – first from contemporary poetry to pre-1900 poetry; and then from poetry to the novel. It is useful at this point just to name the authors whom Leavis found most significant and positive in his account (for a more detailed analysis of what he found to say about each author, see Samson 1992: 108–56). His account of 'the past' of English poetry actually began in *New Bearings in English Poetry* with an introductory sketch of the major Victorian poets and what Leavis saw as their tendency to write 'dream-world' poetry: Browning, Tennyson and Arnold figure prominently in this account. The one Victorian poet who in Leavis's view managed to break free of this tendency was Gerard Manley Hopkins, whose work not only anticipated Eliot's but also remained unpublished until 1918, allowing Leavis to treat him as a kind of honorary twentieth-century poet. *Revaluation*, Leavis's next book on poetry, had chapters on Jonson, Milton, Pope, Johnson, Wordsworth, Shelley and Keats, and included a number of short 'Note' sections on other poets. To simplify drastically, Leavis's argument in *Revaluation* is that (a) most of Milton's writing does not deserve the high status conventionally assigned to it; (b) the most important

English poets of the eighteenth century were (or rather are, since Leavis's emphasis is on which poets can still be read as 'living'): Pope, Johnson, Crabbe and (since he wrote his most important poem in 1797–98) Wordsworth; and (c) of the later Romantic poets Keats achieved more than Shelley or Byron.

Going on to the novel, I do not have to simplify drastically to produce an equivalent summary of what Leavis says in *The Great Tradition*, since he does this himself in his opening sentence:

> The great English novelists are Jane Austen, George Eliot, Henry James and Joseph Conrad – to stop for the moment at that comparatively safe point in history.
>
> (*GT* 1)

We will return to this famous statement later, but it should immediately be noted that Leavis did subsequently add some American names to the list: 'the history of prose fiction in English that I have proposed ... involves the view that if depth, range, and subtlety in the presentment of human experience are the criteria, in the work of the great novelists from Jane Austen to Lawrence – I think of Hawthorne, Dickens, George Eliot, Henry James, Melville, Mark Twain, Conrad – we have a creative achievement that is unsurpassed' (*DHLN*: 17–18). Leavis actually wrote little about Austen, and even less about Hawthorne or Melville, but he did write several essays on Mark Twain (see *AK*). In addition to *Revaluation* and *The Great Tradition*, he also published two miscellaneous collections of other essays on topics in English literary history: *The Common Pursuit* (1952) and *'Anna Karenina' and Other Essays* (1967). Reviewing the contents of these two collections, it is noticeable that the authors covered are mostly the same as the ones covered in the other books. The only significant additions are: Mark Twain, as already mentioned; Jonathan Swift, an author Leavis had written about in his PhD thesis; John Bunyan, who for Leavis was 'a pioneer of the novel' (*AK* 47) and represented the survival of a culture in which it was possible to take pilgrimage seriously; and (a rare venture into literature in translation) the Russian novelist Leo Tolstoy, who Leavis conceded was perhaps an even greater novelist than D. H. Lawrence.

Leavis did not embark on this project of rewriting literary history single-handed; his work was complemented by the work of other *Scrutiny* contributors, as he acknowledged (see Leavis 1968 for his selection of the best of these contributions). The combined effect of all the work was, he later claimed, that *Scrutiny* 'effected something like a revaluation of English literature' (*VC* 229). Leavis also emphasised that '*Scrutiny*'s treatment of the past was scholarly' but insisted that 'the scholarliness was that of the critic who knows what literature is, can recognize it for himself when he finds it, and can discuss it intelligently' (*VC* 229). This interpretation of 'scholarliness' meant that he sometimes went out of his way to *de*-recognise certain authors who he judged did not deserve as much scholarly attention as they traditionally enjoyed. In the first chapter of *The Great Tradition* he puts on an almost comic performance of dismissing a host of much-studied authors: Charlotte Bronte is 'minor'; life is too short to allow much time for reading the novels of Henry Fielding; *Tristram Shandy* is 'irresponsible (and nasty) trifling'. Behind this knockabout stuff there was more than just an intention to shock. Many of Leavis's essays for *Revaluation* and *The Great Tradition* were developed from his teaching, and he believed that it was unrealistic to expect students to make anything of literary history if it was not provisionally organised into a coherent narrative or map. 'Literature is desolatingly vast', as he once put it, and 'it is absurd' that students should be 'flung into a wilderness of books' (*EU* 110 and 47). Leavis's criticism was designed to 'map' the wilderness, pointing out, as it were, the major landmarks and ways to approach them.

The 'map' or navigation metaphor, which Leavis occasionally made explicit (as in the title *New Bearings* ...) and which often features in writing about him, is a useful one for highlighting some of the implications of his approach to literary study. Most of us do find maps useful, and Leavis's bold outlines were welcomed by many students and teachers — particularly in an era when 'English' was a growing subject. In a post-colonial world, nevertheless, we are probably more aware of the ethical ambivalence of maps and mapping, and the implications of both tourism and colonialism that go with them. We can also question Leavis's metaphor in a less politicised way by asking why 'wilderness' should be the appropriate analogy for the multiplicity of interesting different texts that the student is confronted with. Why not a garden? Or indeed the original garden, Eden? Another strong feature of Leavis's criticism which is highlighted by the metaphor of mapping is his interest in *context*. Maps show us where things stand in relation to each other; they encourage us to draw lines between, to 'place', the particular things we encounter separately, and this is what Leavis is constantly doing with the subjects of his criticism (one of the chapters in *Revaluation*, for example, is called 'The Line of Wit'). He habitually searches for links between authors and between texts – even occasionally between particular phrases in different texts. In *Dickens the Novelist,* to take an extreme example, he highlights an 'affinity' between passages in *Little Dorrit* and passages in Blake's poetry, even though he admits he cannot prove that Dickens ever read Blake (*DN* 228). The tendency to construct traditions around individual artists goes with Leavis's fundamental belief that creativity is not dependent on individual genius alone but is essentially *collaborative*. The main focus in *Revaluation* and *The Great Tradition* is on the tradition which should matter most for the critic – the tradition formed by the comparatively rare 'living' or 'great' works. But the habit of networking extends to the construction of more negative traditions as well, such as what Leavis sees as the Flaubertian tradition of privileging technique over human interest (*GT* 8); or the 'disastrous tradition' of thinking of the novel in terms of entertainment rather than serious art (*GT* 153).

'ESSENTIAL DISCRIMINATIONS'? LEAVIS AND CANON-MAKING

If 'map' is relatively benign in its implications, there is another term for what Leavis does with literary history which more immediately focuses its contentious aspects, and that is 'canon'. 'Canon' basically means a list of authors or texts to which a particularly high status has been assigned and from which other authors and texts have been excluded. In recent decades there has been a great deal of public academic debate, particularly in America, over what constitutes the conventionally sanctioned 'canon' of English (and Western) literature. New approaches to literature, and new patterns of readership, have generated immense pressure to add new texts representing different values to the canon. Having a canon at all has come to seem by default an inherently reactionary, repressive practice. But canon-making is exactly what Leavis seems to be doing in the opening sentence of *The Great Tradition*, which is worth quoting again:

> The great English novelists are Jane Austen, George Eliot, Henry James and Joseph Conrad – to stop for the moment at that comparatively safe point in history.
>
> (*GT* 1)

This is perhaps one of the most famous opening sentences of any piece of critical writing. Though it affects bluntness, the statement is in fact highly self-conscious. It depends for its effect on the reader knowing, or guessing, Leavis's reputation, as already established by *Revaluation*:

> Critics have found me narrow, and I have no doubt that my opening proposition, whatever I may say to explain and justify it, will be adduced in reinforcement of their strictures. It passes as fact (in spite of the printed evidence) that I pronounce Milton negligible, dismiss 'the Romantics', and hold that, since Donne, there is no poet we need bother about except Hopkins and Eliot. The view, I suppose, will be as confidently attributed to me that, except Jane Austen, George Eliot, James and Conrad, there are no novelists in English worth reading.
>
> (*GT* 1)

The focus of attention has already shifted here from the great tradition to Leavis himself. The intention, of course, is to ensure that when the idea of the great tradition comes back into focus we pay much more attention to it. What Leavis is in effect doing in this opening section is 'baring the device' of the whole process of canon-making. By being presented with such a bald and apparently uncompromising statement of who the 'great' novelists are, we are forced to think about why we make canons at all. Is there anything to be gained from being less blunt and more conciliatory? According to Leavis, there is much to be lost:

> The only way to escape misrepresentation is never to commit oneself to any critical judgment that makes an impact – that is, never to say anything. I still, however, think that the best way to promote profitable discussion is to be as clear as possible with oneself about what one sees and judges, to try and establish the essential discriminations in the given field of interest, and to state them as clearly as one can (for disagreement, if necessary).
>
> (*GT* 1)

'Discrimination' now has strong legal connotations, of course, and critics of Leavis's canon-making might claim that it is particularly telling that he describes his practice in such terms, since the processes of selection and exclusion which produce a canon all too often turn out to be based on discrimination along class, race, gender or other lines; and the canon itself then becomes part of the system producing and maintaining inequalities along these lines. It is hard to know just what to do with this charge when it is brought against someone whose fundamental prejudices (including norms of class, race, gender, sexuality, etc.) were formed at the end of the nineteenth century, and so are inevitably different from our own in the twenty-first. Several points should be made to put it in perspective at least. First, it is important to note that Leavis was not trying to discourage readers from reading outside the canon he proposed. On the contrary, it is remembered by many of his students that he advised them to 'cultivate promiscuity' (*IM* 163) in their reading – a paradoxical phrase which has interesting implications for the 'wilderness' metaphor mentioned before. Second, selection and exclusion are necessary for any use of language – as Leavis himself notes in the quotation above 'never to commit oneself ... is ... never to say anything'. So if we want to achieve something through the discussion of literary texts a provisional selection of some kind – a canon – is necessary, even if it is not Leavis's canon. Third, we should not overlook the check on 'discrimination' which is built into Leavis's account of the canon-making process: 'disagreement if necessary'. It is easy to discount this as just a formality which Leavis did not take seriously; and it is true that in debate Leavis often responded to disagreement or criticism in a forceful, almost intolerant, style. The point is that, for Leavis, disagreement was not the same thing as agreement to differ: disagreement marked the beginning of engagement in a social process rather than withdrawal from it, and ideally the end of the process was that one view was recognised to be right. Discrimination and disagreement therefore were both premised on the possibility of being, and the responsibility to be, right. This is a basic principle which Leavis reformulated most clearly, long after he had finished with canon-making, in *The Living Principle*: 'My critical judgment is mine ... but ... *my responsibility is to mean it as universally valid*' (*LP* 46; my italics).

THE GREAT TRADITION (1948)

The opening pages of *The Great Tradition* are in some ways a misleading guide to the rest of the book – its title and reputation even more so. It is often thought of as a book which reaffirmed imperial 'Englishness' in a post-war world, but one recent re-reading has suggested that on closer inspection 'Leavis's *Great Tradition* looks less like a rearguard effort of imperial caretaking, and startlingly a bit more like post-colonial criticism *avant la lettre*' (Johnson 2001: 227). In many ways the theme which emerges from the three main chapters is not classical order but rather what Leavis calls 'radical disorder' (*GT* 78); and the book as a whole expresses a set of values in transition, or even conflict, rather than a timeless canon. Leavis's analysis 'strains at the seams' (Robertson 1981: 27); and the tensions which make this so are evident in the way the book was put together. The chapters on George Eliot and Joseph Conrad were originally written for publication in *Scrutiny* in a different order – Conrad first (1941), then Eliot (1945–46). The chapter on Henry James was put together from several different *Scrutiny* essays, published some ten years apart, and this results in some repetition and inconsistency. Leavis discusses Henry James's novel *The Portrait of a Lady* at least twice: one chapter arguing that it is an inferior version of George Eliot's *Daniel Deronda*, in the next restating an earlier view that it is a great work in its own right. The Eliot and Conrad material had not originally been published under the heading of 'the great tradition' but as part of *Scrutiny*'s long-running 'Revaluations' series; and by the time the book was ready for the publishers Leavis had started a new series of essays in *Scrutiny* under the heading 'The Novel as Dramatic Poem'. At a very late stage, when the book was already with the publishers, Leavis decided to include as an additional chapter one of the first essays published under this new heading – on *Hard Times* by Charles Dickens. But this addition has the potential to destabilise the opposition, on which the identification of the 'great tradition' is based, between serious art and Dickensian entertainment. The 'Novel as Dramatic Poem' series later became the main vehicle for Leavis's essays on D. H. Lawrence. So in the addition of the *Hard Times* chapter there is already an indication of a new great tradition forming in Leavis's thought – organised around Dickens and Lawrence and looking back to Blake and Shakespeare. The pre-eminence of the Eliot–James–Conrad tradition enshrined in the book title was already dwindling by the time the book came out: it represents a snapshot of Leavis's thinking at a moment of transition rather than (as the book's first words suggest) his last word on the subject.

That the 'great tradition' should prove open to modification, on the other hand, was still in some sense in keeping with the idea of tradition provided by T. S. Eliot in 'Tradition and the Individual Talent', which as we saw in Chapter 4 ('New Bearings') was a key source for Leavis. Eliot had argued that works of art in a tradition formed an 'ideal order' and it was only by being genuinely individual and new that new works became part of this order, modifying as they did so the whole meaning of the tradition. (There remains the problem that Dickens was not a 'new' author – an issue I discuss in the next section.) The influence of Eliot's model helps to explain why in *The Great Tradition* Leavis makes very little attempt to establish links between the three main authors named in his subtitle. One section does argue in some detail that *The Portrait of a Lady* is modelled on George Eliot's *Daniel Deronda,* but otherwise this is not really a study of tradition in the sense of a line of *influence.* Nor is the tradition to which the three authors belong a matter of shared cultural background or experience – indeed it would be hard to find three nineteenth-century novelists with less shared background than the English George Eliot, the American Henry James and the Polish Joseph Conrad. They do not come from a great tradition but form one. The great tradition really means the tradition of being great – that is, of fulfilling what Leavis regards as the true responsibility of the novelist. This responsibility could perhaps be summarised as to dramatise or make real the way moral questions – questions of how to live well, and more importantly how to fail to live well – are experienced by individuals in human society. Another way of putting this is in the terms Leavis uses to describe a scene he particularly admires in George Eliot's novel *Felix Holt*: 'poignant and convincing … the *implied moral,* which is a matter of the *enacted inevitability,* is that perceived by a psychological *realist'* (*GT* 59; my italics).

Here it is important to note one of the main lines of criticism that has been brought against Leavis's approach in *The Great Tradition* – and not just his approach but the approach that (it is suggested) most readers of novels since Leavis take for granted. This is the critique focused on Leavis's preference for what is called the '*classic realist text'* (see MacCabe 1978; and Belsey 1982). By assuming (so the critique goes) that the work of a great or 'classic' novel is to create the authoritative illusion of a credibly 'real' or 'enacted' world, with a complex but ultimately clear moral structure, the 'classic realist' approach settles for an essentially conservative position. It takes what the narrator says as opening a window on a quasi-real world, and misses the opportunity to discover more subversive things that may be going on in the text – linguistic play or marginal action which subvert the authority of the narrator and make us question what is 'real' or right. Leavis certainly is a 'classic realist' in this sense – there is no getting away from this, even though he was also attentive to linguistic effects and the less obvious features of a text. His approach was, as we have seen, to prioritise – to discriminate – and for him what was most valuable about fiction was the way in which 'enacted inevitability' could deliver an 'implied moral'. What makes his approach more interesting than the standard critique of 'classic realism' suggests is the sense of conflict and precariousness which goes with the recognition of this kind of 'great' achievement. If Leavis was not interested in subverting authority, that was because as he saw it the moral authority achieved by the 'great' novelists was already being subverted – not just by the 'disastrous tradition' in criticism which failed to recognise it, but by the novelists themselves. As Leavis probes the works of his three main authors he finds that each is subject to tendencies that run contrary to the achievement of their best work. So in George Eliot's *Middlemarch* we discover 'a radical disorder' in Eliot's presentation of the story of Dorothea which 'forces us to recognize how intimately her [Eliot's] weakness attends upon her strength' (*GT* 78). In the next chapter he detects what he calls 'inadvertence' in the later Henry James: 'a partial inattention – an inadvertence ... he had lost his full sense of life and let his moral taste slip into abeyance' (*GT* 161). The section of the Conrad chapter on *Nostromo*, which Leavis praises as his most 'Shakespearean' work, concludes by noting 'something radical in Conrad' (*GT* 201) associated with 'a certain emptiness' (*GT* 200) in his vision of life. Analysis of *Nostromo* is immediately followed by *Victory* in which, Leavis suggests, 'life convicts Heyst [the main character] of lack of self-knowledge' (*GT* 203). References to 'lack', 'abeyance', 'self-ignorance' and 'disorder' constitute an underlying theme in the analysis and *The Great Tradition* as a whole can be read as a narrative, encompassing both the authors and their characters, of the struggle to transcend 'lack of self-knowledge' – a struggle which in all but a few great works of art is lost.

DICKENS

Leavis seems vulnerable to the charge of 'lack of self-knowledge' himself when it comes to his dealings with Dickens. There is an apparent change of attitude between *The Great Tradition* (1948) and *Dickens the Novelist* (1970) which is quite striking – and all the more so for being apparently unacknowledged. In the introduction to the earlier book Dickens is deliberately excluded from the great tradition and Leavis states his reasons for this: he recognises that Dickens was a genius but (except in the case of *Hard Times*) 'the genius was that of a great entertainer, and he had for the most part no profounder responsibility as a creative artist than this description suggests ... [t]he adult mind doesn't as a rule find in Dickens a challenge to an unusual and sustained seriousness' (*GT* 19). In the introduction to the later book (co-authored with Q. D. Leavis) this attitude is vehemently denounced: 'We should like to make it impossible ... for any intellectual – academic, journalist or both – to tell us with the familiar easy assurance that Dickens was of course a genius, but that his line was entertainment' (*DN* ix). Dickens is acclaimed by the Leavises as 'the Shakespeare of the novel' and as having 'pre-eminence among English novelists' (*DN* xi). There is a slightly different emphasis in Leavis's own writings in the 1960s and 1970s where D. H. Lawrence is clearly still pre-eminent. But Dickens is nevertheless clearly set up as the great English novelist before Lawrence, and through Dickens a new line is drawn that transcends the conventional genre boundaries: Eliot – James – Conrad is superseded by Shakespeare – Blake – Dickens – Lawrence; a line that represents 'consciousness of responsibility ... responsibility towards life' (*DN* 276).

The emergence of Dickens in Leavis's criticism had begun with the chapter on *Hard Times* first published in 1947; a later essay on *Dombey and Son* was published in 1962, and in 1964 Leavis gave a series of visiting lectures in Oxford on *Little Dorrit*. So the change of attitude was not suddenly revealed in 1970. Even so there was still something embarrassingly abrupt about it for admirers of Leavis's earlier criticism (particularly *The Great Tradition*). Leavis did in fact briefly acknowledge that he had changed his mind: in a footnote to a later edition of *The Great Tradition* (1962) he blamed 'childhood memory and the potent family-reading experience' for his 'absurd' statement about Dickens not challenging the adult mind. But he did not address the question of how the two different traditions he had outlined could be related to each other. If the exclusion of Dickens from 'the great tradition' was 'absurd', how seriously could the rest of the argument of *The Great Tradition* be taken?

The awkwardness of the switch from one tradition to another cannot be made to disappear completely – it is part and parcel of the demands Leavis makes of his ideal 'collaborative reader'. But it is important to note that Leavis's *rapprochement* with Dickens was limited to just three novels – a strong contrast with his writings on Eliot, James and Conrad where a comprehensive sorting of almost all the novels had been offered. The adoption of Blake was even more economical and derived from just a few key quotations. Leavis's use of both Dickens and Blake reflects his sense of the virtue of *opportunism*, which we usually think of as lack of principle but for Leavis meant something more like readiness to express one's principles through creative use of opportunity (creativity and principle being closely associated). As he later wrote of *Scrutiny*: 'we were empirical and opportunist in spirit' (*VC* 221). Dickens lent himself to the later stages of Leavis's career when he was less tied to the demands of the curriculum or of *Scrutiny*, less interested in life as 'enacted inevitability' and more concerned to highlight a stark opposition between life and 'technologico-Benthamism'. The initial template for this opposition is *Hard Times*, with its schematic contrast between the world of the utilitarian Gradgrind and the creative 'Horse-Riding' people whose values are carried into the world of Gradgrind by the child Sissy Jupe. A similar opposition is traced again in Leavis's reading of *Dombey and Son*, where a contrast is worked out between 'money-pride', as represented by the businessman Mr Dombey, and the more life-affirming values of the Toodles family. This broadens out into something much richer and less schematic in Leavis's long essay on *Little Dorrit*, which completes the process of establishing Dickens as the successor to Shakespeare.

SHAKESPEARE

'If one cannot read Shakespeare, then one cannot think' (Leavis 1932: 299). This memorably blunt proposition encapsulates the significance of Shakespeare for Leavis. He later reworked it more diplomatically: 'If you cannot read Shakespeare, then your intelligence has missed an essential training – however rigorous the linguistic, logical and philosophical trainings you may have had' (*EU* 38). But the basic point is the same. Shakespeare's use of language shows us a way of thinking which is more subtle, and which engages more of what it means to be human and belong to a civilised human community, than any other mode of thought.

Leavis found an early opportunity to develop this idea in 1933 when, as noted in the previous chapter, he compared James Joyce's use of language with Shakespeare's. Though Joyce like Shakespeare used language to produce some very complex effects, Leavis judges Joyce's effects to be the result of 'calculating contrivance' while Shakespeare's arise from 'creative compulsion'; Shakespeare's effects 'register the compulsive intensity and completeness with which Shakespeare realizes his imaginative world, the swift immediacy that engages at a point an inexhaustibly subtle organization' (*FC* 210). At the risk of reducing Leavis's approach to another list of 'tags', it is useful to highlight a few key phrases from the above quotations. 'Compulsive intensity' seems to refer to the creative process itself and reminds us again of Leavis's tendency to describe creativity in terms of something which overrides the conscious choosing self ('what *insisted* on being expressed' (*FC* 208)). The phrases 'swift immediacy' and 'completeness' register something similar: the effects are achieved before we have time to think about them ('immediacy') or add anything to them ('completeness'). The quality of 'subtle organization' referred to, finally, is something which seems to belong to both the individual artist and the society which produces him. In Shakespeare's case what made his achievement possible was that he lived in a society which had developed a way of living which combined thought and feeling – an achievement that throws contemporary ways of living into stark relief:

It is an *order* that is gone ... and there are no signs of its replacement by another: the possibility of one that should offer a like richness of life, of *emotional, mental and bodily life in association*, is hardly even imaginable. Instead we have cultural disintegration, mechanical organization and constant rapid change. There is no time for anything to grow, even if it would. If the English people had always been what they are now there would have been no Shakespeare's English ...

(*FC* 217–18; my italics)

The traces of Eliot's concept of the 'dissociation of sensibility' are evident in Leavis's thinking here. Shakespeare represents the undissociated sensibility – proof that it existed once – and as already noted this was one idea of Eliot's that Leavis never rejected. We find him expressing the same idea forty years later, when he claims that if Shakespeare had lived in an age dominated by the demand for 'logic' and 'clarity', 'Shakespeare couldn't have been Shakespeare, and the modern world would have been without the proof that thought of his kind was possible' (*LP* 97).

LEAVIS AND DRAMA

This interpretation of Shakespeare did not require the study of whole plays. Leavis developed it from the close reading of isolated passages (speeches from *Macbeth* were his favourite source) and many of his key statements about Shakespeare are found in essays on more general topics, though he did also write three essays on particular plays (all in *TCP*). Given his concern for the 'living' work of art, it is interesting to note that Leavis expressed in his criticism very little interest in theatrical performance. This is despite the fact that his essay on *Othello* was a recognised influence on one of the most famous twentieth-century productions of the play, in which Sir Laurence Olivier played Othello. Shakespeare is more or less the only dramatist in English literary history Leavis writes about. His maps do not pinpoint any of the other Renaissance or Restoration dramatists, or any nineteenth- or twentieth-century dramatists. The only twentieth-century play Leavis seems to have taken an interest in is T. S. Eliot's verse drama *The Family Reunion* – possibly suspecting a joke at his expense in the name of one of the servant characters (Downing – the name of Leavis's Cambridge college).

Leavis's lack of interest in drama as a genre reflects his lack of interest in *genre* as an organising category generally. The irrelevance of the conventional generic boundaries, between novels, plays and poems, is indicated by the term 'the novel as dramatic poem' in which all three main genres are subsumed. From his point of view all great works of creative writing were *dramatic* in their effect on the reader who was properly attentive. Theatrical performance was just an opportunity for actors and directors to get in the way of this essential critical process. 'How I hate actors' Leavis once wrote, 'being myself histrionic' (*GS* 201). What he did value was reading poetry aloud – indeed in a late lecture he suggested that a poem could not be properly read if it had not been read aloud. Rather than seeing this as a kind of acting, however, Leavis preferred to draw an analogy between reading and playing music: 'Faithfully reading out a poem, a poem that one admires, one should think of oneself as both the violinist and the violin' (*VC* 260).

SUMMARY

Leavis's reading of Eliot and Lawrence determined the way he read everything. But much of his most influential critical writing was on pre-1900 English and American literature, and on the poets and novelists who dominated the traditional curriculum for students of 'English'.

Leavis's approach to literary study was essentially *economic*. He believed it was unproductive to expect students to regard all literary texts as equally valuable (this is not the same as saying one should only read the most valuable). The point of literary study was to distinguish the authors whose work was still 'living' and who represented the living tradition of 'culture' that descended from Shakespeare.

Leavis's reading of English poetry was articulated in *New Bearings in English Poetry* and *Revaluation*; certain key figures represented the Shakespearean tradition but in the nineteenth century, poetry became the vehicle for escape into a dream world. The great nineteenth-century novelists then became 'the successors of Shakespeare'. Leavis at first focused on George Eliot, Henry James and Joseph Conrad as the key figures, but he later found it more appropriate to emphasise Charles Dickens as the representative of this tradition, which culminated in the twentieth century in D. H. Lawrence.

6

CLOSE READING

Leavis is often recognised for his skills as a close reader of texts, even by critics who deplore almost everything else about him. Moreover an emphasis on *close* reading, on the kind of refusal to be distracted by impressive-sounding generalisations which was implied in the journal title *Scrutiny*, is a characteristic of Leavis's work. This chapter therefore offers its own close reading of Leavis as a reader. It looks first at his relation to the 'Practical Criticism' exercise with which he is often identified; then at his own account of what close reading should be; and finally examines two examples of his close reading of poetry.

LEAVIS AND 'PRACTICAL CRITICISM'

For most of the other chapter titles in this book, I have used a term that is prominent and easily found in Leavis's own writings. There is an obvious candidate for this chapter as well – 'Practical Criticism' – a term which has come to be strongly associated with Leavis and can certainly be found in his work. I have deliberately avoided using it, however, for two reasons. One is that Leavis is usually careful to put a certain amount of critical distance between the kind of reading practice he recommends and what 'Practical Criticism' stands for. In *The Living Principle* (1975) he says that he prefers the slightly different formulation 'criticism in practice' (*LP* 19) and though this is not evident in his earlier work it is noticeable that he often puts the term 'Practical Criticism' in inverted commas (*EU* 43). We will probably misunderstand both 'Practical Criticism' and Leavis's approach to reading, then, if we start by treating them as identical. The second reason for not labelling this chapter 'Practical Criticism' is that the term itself, once widely used both formally and informally to describe an exercise in close reading, has tended to fall out of favour as a result of the changes associated with 'Theory'. So not only does it not represent Leavis, it does not directly represent any more what English students are being asked to do. To clarify these distinctions it is useful at this point to review the history of 'Practical Criticism'.

'Practical Criticism' is historically the name of the critical exercise or test used in 'English' in which, often under exam conditions, an individual has to comment in writing on a short passage without the help of any of the additional information resources (name of author, date, previous critical commentary, etc.) which are normally available to a reader. As a test based on a previously 'unseen' text, it is a variation on the translation test sometimes used in the teaching of foreign languages – the variation being that, as the text is already in one's own language, one has to say something else about it rather than just reproduce its exact sense. The use of the exercise was developed in the 1920s by I. A. Richards, during the early years of his involvement in the teaching of English at Cambridge – initially for a prize competition in his college and later as an experimental project with students and colleagues (including Leavis) which resulted in the book *Practical Criticism: A Study of Literary Judgment* (1929). For this project Richards distributed copies of poems without any note of author, date, etc. and asked his students to 'comment freely in writing' on them. He then analysed the returned comments (which he called 'protocols') according to the different kinds of error ('difficulties of criticism') which in his view they exemplified. 'Practical Criticism' soon acquired a momentum of its own detached from Richards. Few readers bothered with the complicated apparatus accompanying his analysis. The book could be used as a kind of test paper in itself as it reproduced the poems Richards had used (the names of the authors were listed at the back in mirror writing so that the reader could not accidentally discover them). The exercise was widely used in schools and universities, particularly as an entrance test. But it remained closely associated with 'Cambridge English' and in 1958 was defended by

E. M. W. Tillyard, a leading figure in the Cambridge English Faculty, on the grounds that 'if properly set, it cannot be faked by the candidate, but, throwing him on his own resources, is a just if severe test of literary perception' (Tillyard 1958: 137). Tillyard's idea of the strength of the exercise highlights what has come to be seen as its weakness in more recent times. Although students are invited to 'comment freely' their freedom is in fact circumscribed by a hidden standard against which their comments will be judged. Because it is difficult to anticipate how an examiner would tell 'faked' from not-faked perception, the exercise looks more like an esoteric power game than a fair test. To avoid this, papers that were once labelled 'Practical Criticism' have sometimes been replaced with course titles which seem more open and less old-fashioned. 'Close Reading' is a useful substitute term in this respect, seeming to suggest no more than the useful forensic skill of being able to attend to detail in any piece of written communication. 'Close reading' still has its ambiguities, however, since 'close' does not just mean 'attentive': it can also mean 'almost right' as in 'not quite, but you're close'.

Leavis's approach was never really the orthodox version of 'Practical Criticism' as just proficiency in close reading. In *Education and the University* (1943) he implies a different use for 'papers of the "Practical Criticism" kind':

> passages of verse and prose to be assigned, on analytic grounds, to period, and also, perhaps, passages to be assigned to their authors. Tests of this kind would be an effective way of insisting on an acquaintance both intelligent and extensive with English Literature. There would also be varied exercises testing perception, judgment and powers of critical analysis.
>
> (*EU* 43)

This is part of Leavis's 'sketch' for an ideal course he never succeeded in setting up, but it corresponds to what is known about his own lectures and seminars, in which typed handouts containing a selection of prose and verse extracts (often called 'dating sheets') were often used. What Leavis would find to say about these extracts is partly reflected in his 'Judgment and Analysis' essays (for a detailed reconstruction of the whole process, and some examples of the sheets, see Page 1995). The exercise was often comparative, and also involved some reference to historical context – assigning texts to periods. So the idea of total isolation of the text from any kind of context does not really correspond to Leavis's approach. What he sought to produce from a close reading was rather a concrete instance of a more general reading of the period – perhaps even (as in *Revaluation*) a narrative of 'tradition and development' *between* periods. Close reading was essentially a way of accessing context rather than cutting oneself off from it.

READING AS 'CREATIVE'/'TOTAL'

The best place to examine Leavis's idea of 'Practical Criticism' is in the chapter entitled 'Literary Studies' in *Education and the University: A Sketch for an English School* (1943). The 'sketch' referred to (which we will look at in more detail in the next chapter) is Leavis's proposal for a final-year degree course, not focused on literature as such but to be taken by students who had had 'the training that "practical criticism" ought to be' (*EU* 69). Having set out this sketch, Leavis devotes the third of his three main chapters, 'Literary Studies', to an account of what this training should involve. The chapter includes several practical demonstrations, but it begins with some general comments on what the analysis of a poem should be like, and from these comments I want to highlight two issues that arise from Leavis's approach to reading – which could be summarised as *creativity* and *totality*. Both arise from the following account of what analysis should be:

> Analysis, one would go on, is the process by which we seek to attain a complete reading of the poem – a reading that approaches as nearly as possible to the perfect reading. There is about it nothing in the nature of 'murdering to dissect,' and suggestions that it can be anything in the nature of laboratory-method misrepresent it entirely. We can have the poem only by an inner kind of possession; it is 'there' for analysis only in so far as we are responding appropriately to the words on the page. In pointing to them (and there is nothing else to point to) what we are doing is to bring into sharp focus, in turn, this, that and the other detail, juncture or relation in our total response ... Analysis is not a dissection of something that is already and passively there. What we call analysis is, of course, a constructive or creative process. It is a more deliberate following-through of that process of creation in response to the poet's words which reading is. It is a re-creation in which, by a considering attentiveness, we ensure a more than ordinary faithfulness and completeness.
> (*EU* 70)

In the sentence beginning 'In pointing to them ... ' we have something like a standard account of what close reading should be – zooming in on 'this, that and the other detail' and perhaps, as implied by 'juncture or relation', cross-referencing this to some other part of the poem or to another poem altogether (Leavis was skilled at doing both). This is perhaps the element in Leavis's performance as a reader that most readers admire, and it seems appropriate that he goes on to describe it as 'creative'. It makes us see things (brings them into 'sharp focus') which we hadn't seen before. It *broadens* the scope for analysis and appreciation, ultimately giving us more to talk about when we talk about the poem. Leavis is not alone in being good at doing this, however. He may have been a brilliant early practitioner of close reading, as were his fellow 'Cambridge critics' William Empson and (in his lectures at least) I. A. Richards. But the stimulating close reading has become a standard set-piece of modern critical writing. Many writers more associated with 'theory' have shown themselves to be wonderful close readers as well. What is more distinctive about Leavis's approach as described in the passage above is the way the creative process is combined with ideas of 'completeness' and 'total response' which seem to set limits to where the process may take us. This comes out even more clearly in another passage later in the chapter, where Leavis is critical of Richards and Empson for (as he sees it) their promotion of the idea that there are no limits to meaning in language:

> Inadequate and naive ideas about the workings of language do without doubt prevail in the academic world and outside, and can profitably receive attention, but there will hardly have been profit on the balance if the literary student, as a result, tends to forget the *one right total meaning that should commonly control his analysis.*
>
> (*EU* 72; my italics)

It is important to recognise what Leavis is *not* saying here. He is not saying that there can be no variety at all in responses to a text; nor is he saying that there can only be one right statement of the meaning of a text. He *is* suggesting, however, that the text has a 'total meaning' and for analysis of the text to be worthwhile this 'total meaning' should be kept in mind – should 'control' the discussion. Here there is clearly much for post-structuralist analysis to get to work on at a theoretical level – querying how the boundaries of the *total* meaning' could ever be marked, for example; or how the *one* ... total meaning' of a text could ever be expressed *as* text without another different 'total meaning' being generated. References to 'control' and 'total' also have political resonances which set alarm bells ringing. But in a different perspective Leavis is just making a pragmatic observation – as implied by his characteristic economic metaphor of 'profit on the balance'. Close reading often takes place in situations where 'control', in the sense of authority, is implicit, whether it is the authority of the teacher, or the examiner, or just the reader's approval. What reading should be oriented towards, Leavis suggests, is not the indefinite proliferation of different responses without any controlling principle, but collaborative agreement on (or at least movement towards) a shared response.

LEAVIS READING JOHNSON

As I have already noted, Leavis's reputation as a brilliant exponent of close reading is enduring. Many critics who find fault with everything else he represents are still prepared to concede that he is worth reading for some of the individual insights he produces in detailed commentary on particular texts. For many admirers, close reading is at the heart of what they admire. Even so, it is not all that easy, browsing through *Revaluation* or *New Bearings*, to isolate impressive examples of *virtuoso* close reading. There is an intermittent, almost teasing, quality to the analysis. Leavis seems again and again to avoid detailed commentary on the text – which perhaps explains why such a high value is sometimes placed on particular detailed observations when they are eventually delivered.

We can see this in the following passage from *Revaluation*, in which Leavis briefly analyses some lines from Samuel Johnson's poem *The Vanity of Human Wishes* (1749). The subject of these particular lines happens to be political power and the futility of chasing after it, but Leavis is not so interested in what Johnson says as in how he says it:

> The process involves a characteristic kind of imagery:
>> For why did Wolsey near the steeps of fate,
>> On weak foundations raise th' enormous weight
> The effect of that is massive; the images are both generalized, and unevadably concrete.

> For such the steady Romans shook the world
>
> -That 'steady' turns the vague *cliché*, 'shook the world,' into the felt percussion of tramping legions.
>
> Unnumber'd suppliants crowd Preferment's gate,
>
> Athirst for wealth, and burning to be great;
>
> Delusive Fortune hears th' incessant call,
>
> They mount, they shine, evaporate, and fall.
>
> The not-too-particularized image of fireworks makes 'burning' something more than the dead current metaphor, and the characteristically Johnsonian 'evaporate' gives the dissipating glory of the rocket with a peculiar concrete felicity.
>
> (*RV* 118)

Here we can see (ironically – in a passage about 'unevadable concreteness') the evasiveness which often appears to characterise Leavis's commentary. On the first lines quoted, for example, he does not attempt to link his statement about 'a characteristic kind of imagery' to particular details in the lines; and when he says 'the effect of that is massive' we are left to work out for ourselves what exactly '*that*' refers to. But when he moves on to the second quotation, he suddenly homes in on one word ('steady') – a familiar word which we might otherwise hardly notice at all as it seems to be there just to make up the required number of stresses in the line. Leavis claims that the effect of this word is that instead of thinking in a fairly vague way about the rise and fall of the Roman empire we get a vivid image – both auditory and visual – of a powerful and disciplined military force on the move, the specific force on which the Roman empire was based. The line looks like a cliché, a conventional formula, but by tweaking one word Leavis makes it appear that there is much more to be got from it. The same is true of the commentary on the final quotation. He spells out something we might have worked out for ourselves (that the would-be politicians rise and fall like 'fireworks') but then avoids spelling out another answer we might reasonably demand – what exactly is 'characteristically Johnsonian' about the word 'evaporate'? Once again we are left to work this out for ourselves. It is worth noting also that in order to bring Johnson's imagery alive Leavis has to use some figurative language of his own. 'Felt percussion of tramping legions' is quite a poetic line in itself – is it really the word 'steady' which gives us the image of the legions or Leavis's own evocation of them? Does the word 'evaporate' have a 'peculiar concrete felicity' – or is Leavis's phrase 'the dissipating glory of the rocket' really doing the work attributed to this word? This is one sense in which Leavis's analysis is, as he says, 'creative'. Many of his best insights, in fact, are like this – often dependent on figurative language for their effect. Another good example is when Leavis describes lines written in imitation of Milton as mounted on 'Miltonic stilts' (*RV* 103); or when he describes the effect of trying to read a poem in a heavily annotated scholarly edition: 'the poem trickles thinly through a desert of apparatus, to disappear time and again from sight' (*TCP* 88).

LEAVIS AND BATESON READING MARVELL

The second instance of close reading I want to look at is one which emerges from an extended debate between Leavis and F. W. Bateson in 1953. The background to this debate is worth noting, as it symbolises at a number of different levels Leavis's position. F. W. Bateson (1901–78) was a lecturer in English Literature at Oxford who described himself as a 'scholar–critic': he respected Leavis's criticism but felt that it needed to be combined with more respect for historical and textual scholarship. In 1951 he had founded a new journal, *Essays in Criticism,* based on the 'scholar–critic' principle; and in the third volume he published an essay, a statement of the journal's 'point of view and programme', entitled 'The Function of Criticism at the Present Time', in which he found fault with a number of modern critics, including Leavis, for the 'irresponsibility' of their careless scholarship (Bateson 1953a: 1,4). Leavis had already contributed a long letter to *Essays in Criticism* clashing with another contributor who had been mildly critical of *Scrutiny*. He now published in *Scrutiny* a crushing reply to Bateson entitled 'The Responsible Critic: or The Function of Criticism at any time', ridiculing Bateson's 'scholar–critic' ideal and his application of it and the pretensions of the new journal to improve on the achievements of *Scrutiny*.

Behind the exchange was a battle between the old and the new journal over which could rightfully claim to be in the Arnoldian tradition ('Essays in Criticism' and 'The Function of Criticism at the Present Time' were the titles of well-known works by Arnold). The traditional rivalry between Oxford and Cambridge perhaps also played a part, although both Bateson and Leavis regarded themselves as outsiders in their respective establishments. But the main battleground was a poem: 'A dialogue between the soul and body' by the seventeenth-century English poet Andrew Marvell (1621–78). In this four-stanza poem, two speakers, 'Soul' and 'Body', take it in turns to complain about their enforced relationship with each other in a living human being. 'Soul', for example, complains of being imprisoned in the body ('hung up, as 'twere, in chains / Of nerves and arteries, and veins'); while 'Body' complains of being forced to stand up and move about by the soul ('A body that could never rest / Since this ill spirit it possessed'). Leavis briefly referred to this poem in *Revaluation*, citing it as an example of the way witty inventiveness could be combined with 'urbanity' (sophistication based on the shared values of a civilised community – see *RV* 74). Bateson identified this as an example of an irresponsible misreading resulting from a lack of awareness of the social and literary context in which the poem was produced.

Bateson's argument is that the poem must be understood in relation to the genre of the 'Emblem Book', popular in the early seventeenth century and particularly associated with the poet Francis Quarles (1592–1644), in which a poem appeared alongside a picture, both illustrating a familiar concept. He cites an actual example from Quarles's *Emblemes* of 'the convention in which Marvell was writing – a skeleton lolling in a sitting posture (the Body) with a kneeling figure inside it (the Soul)' (Bateson 1953b: 319). In Marvell's case, Bateson argues, the use of the convention results in a poem which is *too* visual; we are encouraged to visualise the soul being tortured in the different parts of the body, including the head and heart – but Marvell cannot have meant to suggest that the head and heart were just parts of the body like any other, and so he has ended up saying something he did not mean. Marvell has in effect let the Emblem 'convention' take over his poem; once we know the convention, we realise all that needs to be said about the poem.

Leavis denies the implication that he does not know enough about seventeenth-century literature to read the poem properly; he knows the Emblem Book tradition well enough. But his reading of the poem is that this knowledge does not prevent it being a much greater and more interesting poem than Bateson realises. The poem is not a routine exercise on the soul/body distinction but ('plainly') 'has for theme the *difficulty* of the distinction – its elusiveness' (Leavis 1953a: 169). The precise way in which Marvell articulates the condition of 'Soul' and 'Body' actually prevents us visualising them as separate entities and instead makes us appreciate the nature of what it is to be a living human being, a body that fears to die. He is creatively challenging the conventions rather than simply following them. In this way, by focusing on the poem itself and not allowing knowledge of context to dictate its meaning, Leavis produces a 'remarkably subtle and successful poem'. He ridicules Bateson's 'scholarly method of control' which has the effect of making this much more fruitful reading of the poem 'illicit' (Leavis 1953b: 322–3).

In this instance, then, Leavis's close reading of the poem has had the opposite of a limiting or controlling effect. He has discovered 'illicit' meaning denied by Bateson's more controlling approach; his meaning, moreover, affirms the poet's creativity over his dependence on convention. He has in effect (to recall his terms in 'Literary Studies') made more of a profit from the poem than Bateson – and in these pragmatic, production-oriented terms (as in the Wellek exchange) Leavis is more appealing. This is not the level, of course, at which Leavis justifies his reading – the issue is not, who can do more with the poem, but what is the poem in itself? How do we know the poem? Bateson argues that we can only know the poem by knowing its context: otherwise we are making up the meaning ourselves. Leavis is scornful of this, not because he is not interested in context at all, but because he believes we can only know context through text. In claiming to know the context, Bateson has only come up with 'odds and ends': 'Nothing is plainer than that the arbitrary odds and ends of fact, assumption, and more-or-less historical summary that he produces as "context" serve him merely as licence for not, in any serious sense, reading the poem' (Leavis 1953b: 325). The poem, on the other hand, is 'something determinate – something indubitably *there*' (Leavis 1953a: 174).

Bateson challenged Leavis on this particular phrase, and Leavis recognises that it opens up a theoretical issue, an opportunity for a 'plunge into epistemology' – epistemology meaning the study of how we are able to know anything; in what sense the poem is 'there' for us to know (Leavis 1953b: 325). To a certain extent he tries to get round this by making it appear that the poem's *there*ness is something natural and obvious, so the 'plunge into epistemology' is unnecessary. It is constantly emphasised that Bateson has not looked at the poem properly, has not attended to 'the unequivocal and final evidence of the poem itself' (Leavis 1953a: 170). But he does dip a toe into the epistemological problem in this passage:

> For the reader capable of such recognition the poem is 'there', and the process by which we justify our natural assumption that such a poem can be established as something of common access in which minds can meet, so that if we differ about it our differences are intelligent and profitable, and can perhaps be substantially eliminated, and do not in any case invalidate our convinced working assumption that our perceptions and judgments meet in the poem – this process, comparative and collaborative as it essentially is, demands above all many close and sensitive readings of the text.
>
> (Leavis 1953b: 325)

Though this is not exactly a theoretical argument, it is a useful statement of what is first presented as a 'natural assumption' and then as at least a 'convinced working assumption'. The poem is 'something ... in which minds can meet' (and if they do not meet in the poem there is no chance of them meeting in knowledge of anything less determinate like historical or social context). Leavis would later develop this idea further in the concept of 'the third realm' (see the passage quoted above in 'Key Ideas' Chapter 1) where the meeting is not so much a matter of 'working assumption' as 'necessary faith'.

SUMMARY

'Close reading' for Leavis is the only way in which a text can be read. If we are not attending to particular details, we are not reading the text at all, and it is therefore essential that students, as critics, learn to read attentively and sensitively.

Nevertheless, the point of reading is not to isolate the text from its context but to realise the human situation, and the historical narrative, which is focused in the text.

Close reading is not a systematic but a creative process; the critic's own words play a vital part in making us realise what we are reading.

But close reading is also controlled by the expectation that 'minds can meet' in a shared determination of what the total significance of the text is.

7

ENGLISH, EDUCATION
AND THE UNIVERSITY

Leavis is unique among twentieth-century literary critics in the extent
to which he engaged with ideas about education and universities. Most
teachers of literature, it is true, develop an interest in their profession
and its responsibilities – what is sensible, what is absurd, etc. But
Leavis did not just reflect on how 'English' should be taught; he inte-
grated this with thought on what 'English' was for, and what universities were for ('Why Universities?' Leavis 1934) and he insisted
that these questions were inseparable from the performance of criticism. His key statement on these questions was *Education and the
University* (1943), a book which he hoped would have some influence
on the post-war reconstruction of British education. This chapter
therefore begins by outlining the argument of this book. It then goes
on to explain how Leavis's ideas were shaped by his Cambridge background; and finally considers whether these ideas have any relevance
to the way higher education has developed since the post-war period.

EDUCATION AND THE UNIVERSITY (1943)

Education and the University was the culmination of a series of articles
in *Scrutiny* on different aspects of higher education, some by Leavis
and some by others. The distinctive feature of the book is the 'Sketch
for an English School' (meaning the outline of a university English

course and the community that would be defined by it) in the second chapter. But it is important to understand the overall argument and the problem to which this course is put forward as a solution. As often with Leavis's books, a great deal can be decoded from the title. 'Education' and 'the University' seem to go naturally together, but in fact we will misunderstand Leavis's argument if we assume that the *raison d'être* of a university is to provide education. The idea of a university is rather to be a centre: 'to be, amid the material pressures and dehumanizing complications of the modern world, a focus of humane consciousness, a centre where, faced with the specializations and distractions in which human ends lose themselves, intelligence, bringing to bear a mature sense of values, should apply itself to the problems of civilization' (*EU* 30).

Leavis did not believe that universities had necessarily always had this authoritative role, or even that they were best placed to have it. In his earliest writings he had assumed that the role belonged to the 'minority culture' more generally – intelligent unspecialised critics. But the university was one place where one could still hope to maintain such a centre and bring to focus the cultural tradition that was necessary to resist the machine. The university was the best resource available. Even so, it was vulnerable to the same processes of mechanisation as the rest of the world – in the case of the universities, expressed through too much academic specialisation and not enough 'central' co-ordination.

How could universities be stimulated (Leavis used the unusual word *innervate*) to fulfil their 'central' role? The best way was through 'experiment' and through provision of a course which would focus the attention of staff and students together on the key questions. Leavis was particularly interested in and influenced by a recent attempt to counter the tendency to specialisation and 'departmentalism' in American universities, carried out by the educationalist Alexander Meiklejohn at the University of Wisconsin at Madison. Meiklejohn had set up an 'Experimental College' at which students in their Freshman and Sophomore (First and Second) years had pursued a programme of study comparing America and Athens (see Leavis 1932; Meiklejohn 2001; Nelson 2001). Leavis felt that these two civilisations were too far apart, historically and geographically, to make for a useful comparison and he suggested a better way was to have a course organised around the study of seventeenth-century England and how it differed from twentieth-century England. This is the central element in his proposed 'English School'.

The course Leavis proposed was not really an 'English' course as such. It would perhaps better be described as a programme of Cultural Analysis (but without the elaborate theoretical apparatus that such a title usually connotes): 'it would be a study in concrete terms of the relations between the economic, the political, the moral, the spiritual, religion, art and literature, and would involve a critical pondering of standards and key concepts – order, community, culture, civilization and so on' (*EU* 49). When the 'Sketch' was first published some critics could not see the connection with English at all, but it was there in the reading skills that the students would be expected to bring to the material. As trained readers they would be sensitive to the human element in what they were reading, the spiritual as well as the material. Criticism would be the governing discipline. To explain what he meant by the training the students should have had before they started his proposed course, Leavis added to the book the essay, 'Literary Studies', which we looked at in the last chapter.

Leavis suggested his course could work as an alternative to the final year of the Cambridge English degree course, which included a 'Special Period' paper and a 'Special Subject'. How seriously we take his suggestion foregrounds an important issue. On the one hand, the course outlined in Leavis's 'Sketch' looks like an ideal vehicle for an interdisciplinary or multidisciplinary programme of study. On the other hand it looks like a way to enforce Leavis's reading of the world and the loss of 'Shakespearean' thought in the seventeenth century. To be fair, Leavis did contemplate the possibility of other period-focused studies around which an 'English School' could be organised; his 1950 book *Mill on Bentham and Coleridge*, for example, was intended to be used as a resource for the study of the Victorian period. Even so, one cannot help feeling that his proposals were designed to promote his own reading of history – and that what he meant by the university fulfilling its 'central' role was authorising his own valuations. As Anne Samson has noted in her account of the 'Sketch': 'Here academic freedom seems to reduce itself to finding new ways of agreeing with Leavis's diagnosis of society' (Samson 1992: 82).

Whatever we think of the central scheme, Leavis's sketch has many interesting educational features which are still capable of impressing us as refreshingly sensible innovations. These are not unique insights, but they were in many ways ahead of their time in the 1940s – and arguably still capable of showing up the moribund practices of some institutions today. One feature of Meiklejohn's experiment that Leavis particularly admired was the freedom he had been allowed to reform the whole system of assessment. Leavis saw clearly that how a course is examined determines the nature of the course much more than the content of the lectures. An assessment regime consisting mainly of timed examinations, as most then did, tended to produce the kind of graduate who could be described as 'the complete walking cliché' (Leavis 1950: 3). He recommended instead assessment by coursework, by *viva voce* (interview), and also by students writing book reviews; and he recommended teaching through seminar discussion rather than lectures. He also believed that the education of students would not be complete unless they studied some literature in translation, so his proposed course included compulsory study of Dante and of French and Italian set texts. Another interesting feature of the course is the emphasis on self-direction and incompleteness which Leavis recommends:

> it would be pre-eminently the unacademic virtues that would be demanded and tested: a pioneering spirit; the courage of enormous incompletenesses; the determination to complete the best possible chart with the inevitably patchy and sketchy knowledge that is all one's opportunities permit one to acquire; the judgment and intuition to select drastically yet delicately, and make a little go a long way; the ability to skip and to scamp with wisdom and conscience. There would be some relevant discussions, and the student would be able to consult advisers ... but the work would be a test of his power of self-direction.
>
> (*EU* 60)

He was serious about countering what he called the 'functionless purity' (*EU* 62) of pure specialism or the 'mere obstructiveness' and 'deadness' of strict scholarship (*EU* 59).

It could be objected at this point that incompleteness is all very well when studying cultural history but other subjects require a different approach – what good is 'the courage of enormous incompletenesses' in engineering? Here it is important to remember that Leavis was not recommending his course for all students, but for a self-selecting elite group who could cope with the considerable demands of the course. The point was that such students would help to form a critical 'centre' in relation to which the more specialised work could find its significance. Another criticism levelled at Leavis's proposals when he first published them (and since) was that he did not have an adequate conception of how students who completed his proposed course would be able to influence the world for the better. In fact, if you look carefully at Leavis's proposals it is hard to find anywhere where he specifically claims that his course will produce graduates who *will* change the world, still less that there was anything new about the idea of a course in 'culture' being valuable. He was not inventing the tradition of 'liberal education' – that is, of education as something different from vocational training. He was just seeking to refresh it through a course which was more relevant to the modern world than Classics or Philosophy, the traditional vehicles. It was the maintenance of a 'centre' that was the best reason for having such a course.

LEAVIS AND CAMBRIDGE

To understand Leavis's proposals it is important to consider the context in which he developed them. As we have already seen, an important stimulus came from Leavis's reading about Meiklejohn's Experimental College. Ezra Pound's *How to Read* (dedicated to the President of the University of Wisconsin who had sponsored Meiklejohn's project) provided a similar stimulus, prompting Leavis to write his 1932 pamphlet *How to Teach Reading: A Primer for Ezra Pound*, which contained an early outline of his 'sketch' (reprinted in *EU*). These American sources were important, but a still more important factor was the environment Leavis was working in – Cambridge, England. His proposals in *Education and the University*, though general in principle, were framed in terms of a course that could conceivably be fitted into the existing Cambridge English course structure. One reason for this was to emphasise that the proposals were viable and did not require the creation of a completely new institution or system. Another was presumably that Cambridge was the only university Leavis knew well. But the most important reason was that Leavis believed in Cambridge, and the Cambridge English course, as a 'humane centre' – an institution that represented civilisation's 'recognition of its own nature and needs' (*VC* 222).

To understand why Leavis believed this, it is necessary to know a little more about the history of the Cambridge English course and Leavis's experience of it – although it is also necessary to keep in mind that in the 1960s (after he had retired and his links with Cambridge

were coming under some strain) he was particularly liable to exaggerate or mythologise some aspects of that history. The Cambridge
English course (or *tripos* as Cambridge courses are known) was founded quite late in the day compared with English courses at other
British universities. It did not really exist when Leavis started as a
History student at Cambridge in 1914. When he returned in 1919 it
had just started and he changed from History to English, joining one
of the first cohorts to take the new course, which was at first only
available as part II of the tripos, to be taken after completion of part I
in another subject. Leavis probably enjoyed full exposure, therefore, to
the atmosphere of innovation and special purpose which often attends
the first years of a new course. The delay in setting up the course was
due in part to some fierce debates about what an English course
should be like, and whether English literature was even a suitable
subject for university study. As a result, when it was finally established,
the Cambridge English course had some distinctive characteristics that
are particularly relevant to Leavis's thought. One of these was the
specification, carried over from the recent reform of the Modern
Languages tripos, that students should not just be studying literature
but 'literature, life and thought'. This formula seems potentially a
cliché – one can imagine how it could easily just come to mean a bit
of text and a bit of background. But taken more seriously it encapsulates almost all of what Leavis believed literary study should be
about – not just how people lived and what they thought, but where
the current of 'life' can be traced in the literature of the given period
and how great literature demonstrates what the most important kind
of human 'thought' really is. Another determining influence on the
course was that, when the university's first Professorship in English
Literature was endowed (by the newspaper owner Sir Harold
Harmsworth), it was with the very specific proviso that the professor
should 'treat this subject on literary and critical rather than on philo-
logical and linguistic lines' (see Tillyard 1958: 38). The spirit of this is
directly reproduced in *Education and the University* when Leavis writes:
'Are the principles that should govern a School of English so hard to
grasp? Here, to begin with, is a negative formulation: there is no more
futile study than that which ends with mere knowledge *about* literature' (*EU* 67–8).

Another aspect of the Cambridge environment which helps to
explain Leavis's proposals is the existence of the historic college system

within the university. In Cambridge (as also in Oxford) colleges are semi-autonomous institutions which all students belong to. They organise the recruitment and small-group teaching ('supervision') of students, while the university, through its Faculties and other bodies, organises the lectures and examinations which constitute the tripos. Most lecturers are also fellows of a college (as Leavis was of Downing College from 1936) and each college thus potentially contains within itself a mini-university of fellows from all the different subjects, who work together to manage the affairs of the college – and occasionally even dine together. With this kind of system in the background, one can better understand Leavis's idea of a university as a body with a collective purpose in which the different constituent subjects actively relate to each other (one would not necessarily get such an idea from a large modern institution). The college system also underwrites Leavis's emphasis on the informal milieu created by academic staff and students living and working together: 'Curricula, at the best, give opportunities, and if these are profited by it is mainly owing to the stimulus derived from the general ambience, to the education got in that school of unspecialized intelligence which is created in informal intercourse – intercourse that brings together intellectual appetites from specialisms of all kinds, and from various academic levels' (*EU* 28). Such a milieu or 'ambience' may have been available to the students studying English at Downing College under Leavis – he wrote after the war of 'setting up in the college a stir of life that will act as a kind of vortex' (*VC* 182). But what carried more weight for Leavis was the fact that such a milieu (mainly composed of research students meeting informally at the Leavises' house – see *VC* 219) had actually formed in Cambridge in the 1930s; the proof and the product of such a milieu was *Scrutiny*. Looking back on this development thirty years later, Leavis saw it as representing what he called 'the essential Cambridge'. He famously added 'the essential Cambridge *in spite of Cambridge*' (*NSMS* 63; my italics). This is partly intended as a reproach to Cambridge, a reminder that *Scrutiny* had come into being just as Leavis had found himself without a lecturing post in the university (see the box below for a more detailed account of this). But on a less personal level it also expresses the idea that what a university represents, what it is in its *essence*, can be detached from the negative connotations of 'academic' institutionalisation.

LEAVIS AND THE CAMBRIDGE ENGLISH FACULTY

Recognition of Leavis's stature as a critic is sometimes linked to the idea that in his own university and department (Faculty) he had to contend with unjust treatment and *lack* of recognition, particularly when it came to appointment and promotion. Even T. S. Eliot apparently commented on the 'difficulties' he understood Leavis had experienced at Cambridge (*IM* 244). But it has never been a straightforward matter to weigh how serious, or how unjustly caused, these 'difficulties' were. The documented facts alone can't really settle this, but it is better to know exactly what they are (as recorded in the *Cambridge University Reporter*):

- When Leavis started lecturing in Cambridge, in the early 1920s, he and almost all his colleagues worked on a freelance basis (paid per student).
- In 1926 the teaching system was restructured: the longer-serving lecturers were confirmed in permanent salaried posts designated University Lectureships, while those who had started lecturing more recently, including Leavis, were appointed to junior fixed-term posts designated Probationary Faculty Lectureships.
- Leavis's fixed term as a Probationary Faculty Lecturer expired in 1931–32; he was then without a university post and had to wait in hope that he would be appointed to a University Lectureship when one became vacant.
- Between 1931 and 1936 several vacancies came up but went to other people younger than Leavis. He was finally appointed to a University Lectureship in 1936, but it was on a 'Part Work' basis – what today would be described as a 0.5 post.
- In 1946 his post was upgraded to full-time; and in 1959 he was appointed to the more senior post of University Reader, from which he retired in 1962.

The two elements in the above which could be taken as possible evidence of unfair treatment are: being passed over for appointment to a permanent post in the early 1930s; and being kept on 'part work' for ten years after that. A third issue is that Leavis also complained of being politically disadvantaged within the Faculty: 'I was, in my academic career (if that is the word), made to feel irretrievably an outlaw, and I remained to the end conscious of being looked on by those in power as a deplorable influence'(*LC* 147). It is more difficult to find evidence for this kind of claim – and even if it could be found, it could be argued that what Leavis describes is not injustice so much as the inevitable politics of any self-governing organisation. Leavis and his enemies both played for power, but in different ways – and in the longer perspective, in terms of who commanded public attention, sold books, and is now remembered as a great Cambridge figure, it is not clear that Leavis was the loser.

'EXTENDING HIGHER EDUCATION TO THE UTMOST'?

Education and the University was politely reviewed, but it did not really play any part in post-war developments as Leavis had hoped – either in Cambridge or in British Higher Education more generally. In the period immediately after the war, the idea dominating university expansion was that the country needed more scientists. The government did provide funding for one major experiment in a new kind of university college at Keele in North Staffordshire, which opened in 1950. But the discipline that was supposed to act as a central reference point for all the different subjects in the new course there was not literary criticism but philosophy. Towards the end of the 1950s, much greater funding was released for the development of a number of completely new universities, which opened in the early 1960s. But these institutions tended to promote the social sciences as their 'centre'. Leavis still directed his own mini-version of an 'English School' at Downing College, and secured some funding from the Rockefeller Foundation to help build up a 'vortex' there. But he could only control teaching and admissions – not the curriculum. He often encouraged his students to change to another subject for the second part of their degree, and many did, remaining in touch with the literary–critical 'centre' through Leavis's college seminars, which they were still able to attend. Leavis's aim was not that more people should study English literature but that a literary training should play more of a part in what other people studied. In this sense, although English became a very popular subject during the post-war period (as it still is), he did not see his ideas realised.

British Higher Education has been transformed several times over since 1943 and it is worth looking more closely at whether Leavis's thinking has any bearing on these changes. In the 1960s there were many tensions, and changes, due to unprecedented expansion. The new universities were one form this expansion took. But there was a more general increase in student and staff numbers in response to the problem of increased demand for places, demand caused by a temporary bulge in population and also a long-term trend resulting from post-war changes in secondary education. The problem was addressed by the famous Robbins Report (named after the economist Lord Robbins who chaired the reporting committee) which recommended that funding should be increased so that there was a university place available for everyone who could benefit from it. This led to increased spending on existing universities, as Robbins had recommended. But later it also led – more controversially, and against what Robbins had recommended – to development of what came to be known as the 'binary policy' for higher education, whereby some of the necessary expansion was achieved not through universities but through the development of other kinds of local institutions – polytechnics and colleges – which were funded and organised differently. Leavis contributed quite forcefully to the debate about these changes, through letters and lectures, seeing in the expansion of numbers an extension of the 'technologico-Benthamism' that C. P. Snow had represented and adding Lord Robbins to his list of hated 'Snow-men'. But in practice his polemics did not engage very effectively with the two main topics of debate – expansion and the binary policy. He declared he was '*in favour of extending higher education to the utmost*' (*NSMS* 150; his italics) but added that it was 'disastrous to identify higher education with the university ... A university can't be adequately conceived in terms of what the word "education" ordinarily suggests; a real university is a creative centre of civilization' (*NSMS* 151). Leavis was here restating one of the main points of *Education and the University*, but by distinguishing *higher education* from *the university* at this moment he seemed briefly to be endorsing the binary policy. He was not really in favour of any current policy because he did not recognise the situation that had produced the increased demand. But by being against expansion generally he was understood to be in sympathy with the slogan 'More Means Worse', even though this was originally formulated by the novelist Kingsley Amis, a figure Leavis abhorred. The true university hardly existed anywhere, on either side of the divide, although Leavis did claim he had discovered it at the University of York, where after his retirement from Cambridge he became a Visiting Professor (*NSMS* 193; and see Storer 1995a).

In the 1980s British Higher Education went through a period of cuts in funding, sometimes dubbed 'Snibborism' – Robbins in reverse. But this has been followed since the 1990s by a renewed drive towards what is sometimes called 'Mass Higher Education', with targets for increased participation that dwarf the relatively modest expansions of the 1960s. At the same time the end of the 'binary policy' cleared the way for former polytechnics and colleges to be rebranded as universities – and for all institutions to compete more desperately with each other for funding, status and students. Many institutions have grown and developed in this environment, but many changes have come with it. Two changes that seem particularly at odds with Leavis's ideas are that with more publicly funded growth has come (a) a much greater emphasis on justifying higher education in terms of how it contributes to the local and national economy; and (b) a pervasive 'audit culture' which constantly requires students and teachers to describe their learning in terms quite alien to the particular subject they are studying; and vests academic authority in external standards rather than the shared culture of an academic community.

The cultural historian Joe Moran has described these kinds of effects as 'the discourse of managerial instrumentalism' and has considered in some detail whether Leavis's writings counter this discourse in any way. His conclusion is that they do, but only in a limited sense – essentially because (as in the 1960s) Leavis's model of what a university should be is so small-scale (and therefore apparently exclusive):

> We obviously cannot return to Leavis's elitism, or his certainties about the central role of English within the university ... But it is also true that Leavis's idea of the university as a separate space responds to real external challenges facing both English and the university which have become even more pressing in recent years. His work represents perhaps the last well-coordinated response to these challenges, largely because university English in its present formulation has struggled to develop an oppositional idea of the university and its own role within it.

(Moran 2002: 11)

What this suggests is that there is some residual value in Leavis's ideas inasmuch as they are at least oppositional. Some of the specific criticisms that Leavis brought against earlier versions of the system, as I have already suggested, certainly still apply to present conditions. Contemplating the effect of increased numbers of students, for example, Leavis asked a question that has been asked many times since: 'When are they [university teachers] supposed to get their own reading and thinking – what one may properly refer to as their own creative work (for it should be that) – done?' (*NSMS* 155). Leavis's phrase 'the complete walking cliché' also seems apt to the discourse of managerialism, which has a tendency to make such clichés of all students and staff – endlessly circulating bland assurances about 'quality', 'excellence' and 'satisfaction' in a manner that does not seem to have much to do with critical thinking. If we want to bring Leavis's ideas to bear more positively, however, we have to go back to the 'sketch' in *Education and the University* and consider whether we can imagine anything like his course, and its role in facilitating a 'creative centre', being realised in the present system. At a superficial level this is in fact surprisingly easy to envisage. Everywhere you look, in the UK higher education sector at least, institutions have set up small-scale 'centres', focused on particular areas of study within the arts and social sciences. These often have supporting MA programmes attached; and an MA, rather than an English first degree course, is probably the closest modern equivalent to the demanding second part of a degree that Leavis proposed. Such projects are often structured in ways similar to the experiment Leavis proposed. It is much harder to imagine, however, that in a university of contemporary 'mass' proportions and ethos, a 'centre' could ever assume the 'central', difference-making, role Leavis envisaged for it. The real test, moreover, of whether such centres replicate Leavis's experiment must be whether they genuinely succeed in fostering a 'creative' milieu out of which could emerge a critical discourse like that of *Scrutiny*, commanding public interest and respect in the way Leavis believed *Scrutiny* had. This last condition is a particularly tall order. But Leavis believed in the creative potential of 'opportunism'. Interpreted in such a spirit, it is possible that Leavis's proposals might still prove more inspirational, and practically relevant, in the present situation, than is usually assumed.

SUMMARY

For Leavis, a university exists primarily not to provide education but to be an authoritative centre of critical thinking about society and its values.

One way to encourage such a centre to form is through staff and students working together on the kind of experimental course outlined in Leavis's 'Sketch'. The role of 'English' would be to prepare students for such a course.

Cambridge provided the model environment for Leavis's proposals because it was collegiate and the English course encouraged an experimental approach to the study of 'life and thought'. Post-war developments in higher education did not allow any opportunity for Leavis's ideas to be implemented, but his ideas still have potential relevance to the contemporary situation.

8

'LIFE'

Chapters headed 'Life' usually come near the beginning of books like this. To avoid confusion I have moved this one towards the end because it is not about Leavis's life as such – what is particularly relevant to know about that has already been outlined in previous chapters – but about his unusually emphatic use of 'life' as a positive term in his writing. It starts by looking at an example of the way Leavis introduces 'life' into a discussion; it then notes some different ways he refers to 'life' in his criticism; and concludes by considering whether his repeated invocation of 'life' as an ultimate value means he should be considered a religious writer.

'A NECESSARY WORD'?

In a recent essay reflecting on Leavis and 'theory', John Schad describes Leavis as 'the Cambridge critic who from the forties to the sixties dominated literary criticism with his reverential and enigmatic talk of "life" ... To this day, within literary criticism, "life" means "Leavis" and "Leavis" means "life"' (Schad 2003: 168). It is interesting that in this kind of description, as in my chapter heading, one feels that 'life' should be in inverted commas. Leavis in a sense always wanted to rescue 'life' from being enclosed in this way – from always appearing to be a quotation, someone else's concept and responsibility. This is illustrated by an anecdote that he told in the first of his 1967

Clark Lectures at Cambridge. Leavis describes how, after listening to a paper on the subject of the idea of a university, he opened the discussion by suggesting that the term 'life' could be substituted for what the speaker had called 'continuity' or 'tradition':

> The reader of the paper saw my point, but as I expected, it wasn't taken up in discussion. But towards the close a speaker who had shown himself notably articulate remarked, glancing back over what had been said, that I, he gathered, was a vitalist. I could only reply that I didn't see how that word helped. I felt, in fact, non-plussed; very few, it was plain, had taken my meaning, and I recognized that an attempt to convey it on that kind of occasion was an enterprise absurdly out of the question. No thought of any philosophy or intellectual system, of course, had been in my mind; I merely meant to evoke in my hearers a strong present sense of what they of course knew, and to insist on its crucial relevance.

(ELTU 53–4)

This is typical of the occasional anecdotes which have an important rhetorical function in Leavis's later writing (in this one sense life and 'life' went together). Their purpose is almost always to demonstrate the difficulty of getting other people to recognise the urgency of the problems Leavis is trying to address – the difficulty being an index of how bad the problem is ('as I expected, it wasn't taken up ... very few, it was plain, had taken my meaning ... '). A related feature of such anecdotes is that Leavis often presents himself as struggling to communicate while his opponent is 'articulate'. In this case the story actually has many resonances with the 1937 exchange with Wellek that we looked at in detail in 'Key Ideas' Chapter 2. In his second contribution to this exchange, Wellek had noted that, for all Leavis's evasions, 'it is clear from your reply that "vitality", "Life" etc, seems your highest value, a concept which obviously opens all sorts of difficult questions ... ' Leavis must have felt, in the situation he describes here, that he was meeting the spirit of Wellek yet again, since the anecdote strongly recalls Wellek's parting shot in 1937 and illuminates Leavis's response to it. The articulate speaker, like Wellek, had attempted to identify Leavis with a particular 'philosophy or intellectual system' – in effect a theory – based on 'Life' and its synonyms. Leavis again rejects this as a redundant and meaningless exercise – 'I didn't see how that word helped'. But the word 'vitalist' must have been specifically intended to 'help', by distinguishing one particular 'intellectual system' from a range of others. It is exactly this process of differentiation, however, implying a range of alternatives to 'talk of "life"', which Leavis denies. His interpretation is not grounded on a particular system but on what he represents (enforcing it with a double 'of course') as a universal condition ('what they of course knew'). Taking refuge in the word 'vitalism', like putting 'life' in inverted commas, is just avoiding what you know – and seems to go with the suggestion that there is something morally evasive about being too 'articulate' in these matters. 'All important words are dangerous', Leavis wrote around the same time (*LA* 51) – and 'life' was 'a necessary word' (*DN* 217).

'LIFE' IN LANGUAGE

In his close reading of texts, Leavis often describes the way language works in terms of 'life' or 'livingness'. In his essay on 'Literary Studies', for example, which we looked at in 'Key Ideas' Chapter 6, his first practical demonstration of criticism in practice is an analysis of Matthew Arnold's sonnet 'To Shakespeare'. His overall judgement of this poem is that it shows Arnold wanting to write great (Shakespearean) poetry but failing to do so. If we look more closely at the terms in which he develops this judgement, we can see that his valuations are based on a set of opposed terms: particular/general; inside/outside; present/absent; realised/unrealised; alive/dead. Seizing on the image in the fifth line of the poem, for example, he claims it 'could only have been offered by an *unrealizing* mind, handling *words from the outside*' (*EU* 74); he later refers to the same image as indicating 'a radical *absence* of *grasp*' (*EU* 76), and notes 'a general debility that is manifested throughout the sonnet in the *dead* conventionality of the phrasing – in the lack of any *vital* organization among the words' (*EU* 76); Shakespeare's genius, on the other hand, is praised for the '*inwardness* and completeness of its humanity'(*EU* 75) [my italics]. The implication is that, while all poetry is made of words, good poetry presents both the reader and the author with something which has an organic life and physical presence of its own – something we can 'grasp' and with which we can be intimate. Words become, in other words, living things. This is an appealing way of describing language, but it is *metaphorical* – words are not literally 'alive' or physically 'there' in space – and it could be argued that, by describing the text as if it were a body which the critic has to check for signs of life, Leavis is avoiding more difficult questions about how language works.

It is slightly more complicated than this, however, because where Leavis does refer to 'life' and 'presence' in his analysis of texts he often uses this to confront us with thought about what 'life' and 'presence' actually mean. One such analysis, as we have seen (Chapter 6 again) is his reading of Marvell's 'Dialogue between the Soul and the Body', which Leavis admires precisely because of the way, as he sees it, the poem presents us with the *difficulty* of thinking about the soul as separate from the body; thus making us realise something about what being sentient and alive is like. Another important set-piece analysis, which Leavis used in his teaching and which appears in *Revaluation* and is also alluded to in the reading of the Marvell poem, is one based on some lines from Shakespeare's *Measure for Measure* (III.1.117), in which the character Claudio tries to imagine in physical terms what it is like to die: 'Ay, but to die, and go we know not where; / To lie in cold obstruction and to rot … '. Leavis compares the 'vivid concreteness of realisation' in Shakespeare's lines with the 'wordy emotional generality' of some very similar lines from the poet Shelley's verse drama *The Cenci* (*RV* 225–7). Shakespeare's lines are 'vivid' (from the Latin *vivere* = to live) in more senses than one. Not only do they *seem* to realise or bring something to life, but *what* they bring to life is the nature of sentient life itself: 'Sentience, warmth and motion, the essentials of being alive … recoil from death'. Claudio's speech is referred to again in Leavis's essay on *Measure for Measure* (in *TCP*), where Leavis suggests it plays its part in the affirmation of 'life' which the entire play is about. It is particularly an answer to the long speech by the Duke (disguised as a Friar) earlier in the same scene, in which Claudio is advised to discount life and be 'absolute for death' (III.1.5). As long as one is alive, Leavis suggests, one cannot sincerely adopt this attitude to the negation of life.

'LIFE' AS 'REALITY OF THE SPIRIT'

Leavis's invocations of 'life' seem to epitomise what in the first chapter of this book I called the 'monstrosity' of his criticism. How can a word which has so many different uses, and gestures so generally towards the whole of existence, be managed in a disciplined way in intellectual discussion? On the other hand, Leavis's use of such a term can be compared to the key terms used by some other thinkers. It has been likened, for example, to the term *Lebenswelt* (life-world) which was particularly important for the phenomenologist Edmund Husserl (see Poole 1996: 391); also to the term *Erlebnis* (lived experience) used by the German philosopher Dilthey (see Bell 2007: 201). Every thinker perhaps has a word of ultimate power like 'life' in their critical vocabulary. It is the 'dangerous' way Leavis handles his word that makes his use of it more problematic.

In fact one can easily exaggerate the extent to which Leavis invoked 'life'. Wellek may have recognised its importance for Leavis early on, but 'life' does not have quite the same profile in his earlier writings as it does in, for example, his later essays on Dickens and Blake. In 'Mass Civilisation and Minority Culture' (1930), as we have seen, Leavis appealed to 'the implicit standards that order the finer living of an age' and equated 'fine living' with 'distinction of spirit' – phrases which in retrospect take on connotations (perhaps not entirely unintended on Leavis's part) of country house parties and the social world of the English aristocracy. In the introduction to *The Great Tradition* (1948) he refers tentatively to 'human awareness … awareness of the possibilities of life' as what makes 'the few really great' authors significant (*GT* 2). This formula seems modelled on Matthew Arnold's description of poetry as 'criticism of life' and goes with the emphasis in *The Great Tradition* on 'enacted inevitability'. The great novelists show us the complexity of life, not only its possibilities but also its more tragic inevitabilities. By the time he came to write his essay on Dickens's *Little Dorrit* in the 1960s, Leavis had moved on from this relatively muted invocation of 'life' to something much more rhapsodic: 'life, the spontaneous, the real, the creative … ' (*DN* 215). This is the stage at which Leavis seems to come closest to being describable as a religious thinker, and the essay on *Little Dorrit* is particularly rich in instances of Leavis's use of 'life'. There are examples here as elsewhere of 'life' as a quality attributed to Dickens's use of language. But above all the emphasis is on 'life' as something to be vindicated – vindicated first by Dickens, confronting his society, and then by Leavis: 'Life always has to be defended, vindicated and asserted against Government, bureaucracy and organization – against society in that sense' (*DN* 262).

The essay on *Little Dorrit* is probably the longest Leavis ever wrote on just one text. His basic method, though far from crudely schematic, is to consider the different characters and the part each plays – for or against – in the overall 'affirmation of life' which the whole novel is. 'The affirmation is of life, which – this is the insistence – doesn't belong to the quantitative order, can't be averaged, gives no hold for statistics, and can't be weighed against money' (*DN* 224). This way of evoking 'life' negatively, by its property of *not* being reducible to material quantities, does not have to be considered particularly religious. But at one point in the analysis Leavis goes out of his way to suggest that it should be described in this way. He notes that at a climactic moment in the narrative (the exposure of the society swindler Merdle) Dickens imagines the scene being perceived by 'a solitary watcher on the gallery above the Dome of St Paul's' (the Cathedral in the City of London). This passing detail, Leavis suggests, is not 'just convention' but symbolises 'institutional religion' and in a spirit which transcends the satire on institutions which runs through the novel. St Paul's stands for 'a reality of the spirit, a testimony, a reality of experience, that, although it is a reality of the individual experience or not one at all, is more than merely personal'. Leavis notes that in the next paragraph Dickens includes several allusions to the New Testament and concludes that the effect of this is 'to emphasize how essentially the spiritual, in what no one could fail to recognize as a religious sense, is involved in the whole evocation' (*DN* 270). This corresponds to another passage in Leavis's later writing, often quoted, where he again suggests that great literature is characterised by being 'religious' in its effect: 'In coming to terms with great literature we discover what at bottom we really believe. What for – what ultimately for? What do men live by? – the questions work and tell at what I can only call a religious depth of thought and feeling' (*NSMS* 56). To illustrate what he means by 'religious' in this case, Leavis characteristically invokes D. H. Lawrence: 'Perhaps, with my eye on the adjective, I may just recall for you Tom Brangwen, in *The Rainbow*, watching by the fold in lambing-time under the night-sky: "He knew he did not belong to himself"'. The same Lawrence quotation (whose use we also noted in Chapter 2) appears only a few paragraphs earlier in the essay on *Little Dorrit*.

SUMMARY

For Leavis, 'life' cannot be summarised. Nor can it be reduced to a term in a theoretical system.

'Life' is a property of language when it is used creatively. But it is also what the creative use of language makes us realise – what it is like to be alive.

'Life' means the shared experience of past human 'living'; it is what makes individual lives matter; it is what we have a 'religious sense' for; it is what great works of art exist to affirm.

AFTER LEAVIS

The decisively new and unforeseen may yet reward us.

(Leavis 1976: 156)

Let me just add something which has to do with the language: 'to follow' in French is suivre *and when I say 'I follow' in French, I say* je suis *which also means 'I am' so it complicates, it complicates the grammar.*

(Derrida 2003: 14)

There are two ways of approaching the subject of this chapter. One is historical – to tell the story of what happened after Leavis. The other is critical – to attempt what Leavis called 'revaluation'. What is the status and relevance of Leavis now, in relation to the various issues with which he engaged? Can he still do anything for us? I will return to these questions at the end, but will begin with the story. There are two ways of approaching this as well, since to the question 'What came after Leavis?' there are two obvious answers. One is that after Leavis came 'Leavisites'. The other is that after Leavis came something else – the changes associated with 'theory'.

AFTER LEAVIS (1): 'LEAVISITES'

For some of the thinkers in this series it is possible to say that their influence only began to be felt as a significant force after their death.

This could be said, for example, of the international profile of the Russian linguistic theorist Mikhail Bakhtin (1895–1975), who happens to have been an exact contemporary of Leavis. In Leavis's own case the opposite is true. The phenomenon of his influence and his followers (dubbed 'Levites' or 'Scrutineers' in the 1930s, until the term 'Leavisite' became more common) was part of his profile from the start. It has always played a part in the way he has been discussed. In a sense it goes with the emphasis on tradition, and on *collaboration*, which plays such an important part in his thinking. Leavis was able to a certain extent to create a small community through his role as Director of Studies for English at Downing – and to create a larger one through liaison with the school teachers who prepared potential students for the entrance examinations that he controlled (for an account of how this system worked see MacKillop 1995: 53–66). But more important was the idea (and for a while the actual existence) of an informal 'centre' – a group made up not just of students but of teachers, researchers and critics who would create the *milieu* which in turn would produce and sustain a journal like *Scrutiny*. Publication of *Scrutiny* came to an abrupt end in 1953 when Leavis realised he no longer had an adequate network of contributors – a viable centre – to keep it going. But he continued to emphasise, throughout the rest of his career, the need for another vehicle which could recover *Scrutiny*'s role.

The story of 'after Leavis' is partly the story of attempts to establish such vehicles. Several journals were set up in the 1950s which set an agenda to take the best of Leavis's practice and improve on it in some way. I have already mentioned F. W. Bateson's journal *Essays in Criticism* (started in 1951) which aimed to provide a more scholarly version of *Scrutiny*. *Critical Quarterly*, which was launched in 1959, was also intended as a successor to *Scrutiny* and included in its first volume a symposium on 'Our Debt to Dr Leavis'. Another initiative of the 1950s was *The Pelican Guides to English Literature*, an influential series of multi-authored guides to periods of English literary history which were widely used as textbooks by teachers and students. Many former *Scrutiny* authors contributed to this series, which was edited by Boris Ford, one of Leavis's particularly enterprising former Downing students. Yet Leavis was equivocal about the initiative, declined to contribute personally to the *Pelican Guides*, and apparently saw them as a contributing factor in the demise of *Scrutiny*. Ford himself later wrote with regret of Leavis being reluctant to broaden his audience (Ford 1984: 110). A similar pattern of new initiatives failing to secure Leavis's recognition was repeated in the 1960s when a group of Leavis's closest associates set up a new journal, with a clear allusion to *Scrutiny* in its title *The Cambridge Quarterly*, and also raised funds to endow an 'F. R. Leavis Lectureship' at Cambridge so that Leavis would have at least one recognised successor at Cambridge following his retirement in 1962. These initiatives seemed at first to enjoy Leavis's support but before long there was a traumatic break between him and the group (though the journal itself, like *Essays in Criticism* and *Critical Quarterly*, survived and is still thriving). Leavis later contributed some articles to another new journal with the explicitly Leavisite title *The Human World* but this only ran for four years, although it was reincarnated for a while in the 1980s as *The Gadfly* and in various other ventures published by the Brynmill Press, founded by another former student of Leavis.

The problem faced by all these initiatives was how to resemble *Scrutiny* without redundantly repeating all the same valuations and covering the same topics – in other words how to negotiate the complicated grammar, pointed out by Derrida, of being and following. Since it was impossible to *be* Leavis, to follow him meant *not to be* Leavis, to be different from him. But at this point there was the inevitable risk of not being recognised by Leavis – as Raymond Williams anticipated when he opened his contribution to the *Critical Quarterly* symposium: 'We must try to pay our debt to F. R. Leavis, *whether or not he will acknowledge us as debtors*' (Williams 1959: 245; my italics). What all would-be 'successors' came up against was the unresolved tension in Leavis's thinking between what he saw as the two key principles of creativity sustaining the 'human world' – collaboration but also 'intransigence' (*CAP* 40). He did not really have an answer to how, in practical politics, these two could be reconciled. As Michael Bell observes, it was 'in the nature of his critical vision that the collaborative community was so much, and tragically, in his own mind' (Bell 2000: 422).

It is important to tell this story in terms of the difficulty of reproducing Leavis's criticism, because often the assumption is that it was all too reproducible ('widely disseminated' as I said in my first chapter). There is sometimes a suggestion that the 'Leavisites' were a tightly organised group who took over the teaching of English in schools and universities and ran it on Leavis's instructions. An *Observer* article in the 1960s even offered to expose 'the hidden network of the Leavisites'. It is not too surprising, perhaps, that the 'Leavisites' have been imagined in this way, since this was how Leavis himself imagined other networks of influence, such as 'Bloomsbury' or 'the literary establishment', extending their power. But it is a misleading picture, both as it applies to the various initiatives mentioned in the last paragraph and to the more general phenomenon of generations of students going on from Leavis's Cambridge to careers in the world beyond Cambridge. It is true that *Scrutiny* initially encouraged graduates to think of teaching as a kind of mission field for 'culture and environment' work; and that many of Leavis's students became influential teachers. Many also worked in higher education, not just in English but in Education departments, where they also influenced teachers. So some elaborate family trees or spider-web diagrams of 'Leavisite' lines can be drawn up (see Ball 1987, for example). But we should be wary of thinking that these relationships convert into some kind of block vote for Leavis. To take an extreme example, one of Leavis's students at Downing was Philip Hobsbaum, who later became a very influential figure amongst a group of modern poets (confusingly known as 'The Group') and an important innovator in the development of creative writing within English departments. Hobsbaum also spent several years as a teacher in a secondary school in South London, where one of his pupils was Ken Livingstone, later Mayor of London and one of the most controversial and high-profile figures in British politics, who has testified that Hobsbaum was the teacher who 'made a difference' in his life. We could thus in theory claim 'The Group', creative writing courses, *and* Ken Livingstone's management of London, as markers of the spread of Leavis's network of influence – but of course this would be absurd. The reality is that it is always difficult to assess the influence of any one teacher, Leavis or 'Leavisite', so many other factors being involved. For some it was a decisive influence; for others what was more decisive was their reaction against Leavis; for others there were other more important influences. This would probably be particularly true of the quite large number of Cambridge English students whom Leavis taught, or who have recalled the strong impression he made on them, who later went on to careers in the creative arts, such as the theatre directors Peter Hall and Trevor Nunn; the playwright Simon Gray; the novelists Howard Jacobson and A. S. Byatt; or the poets D. J. Enright and Donald Davie. It would be interesting to examine their work for signs of what it meant to them to be 'after Leavis'. But the signs would not constitute a secret 'Leavisite' code. Their way of following Leavis, consciously or unconsciously, must necessarily have been to find a way of being different from him.

AFTER LEAVIS (2) 'THEORY'

Much of what I have said so far has been about Leavis's influence on those he had direct contact with. But the more significant question must be what difference Leavis's writings made to the majority of students and readers who (like myself) never met or had anything to do with him during his lifetime. When *Scrutiny* closed in 1953 Leavis blamed it on his 'utter defeat at Cambridge' (quoted in Jameson 1970: 297). But thirty years later the critic Terry Eagleton estimated that in the wider world Leavis and *Scrutiny* had secured 'victory' by establishing a universal model of what 'English' was about:

> Far from constituting some amateur or impressionistic enterprise, English was an arena in which the most fundamental questions of human existence – what it meant to be a person, to engage in significant relationship with others, to live from the vital centre of the most essential values – were thrown into vivid relief and made the object of the most intensive scrutiny. *Scrutiny* was the title of the critical journal launched in 1932 by the Leavises, which has yet to be surpassed in its tenacious devotion to the moral centrality of English studies, their crucial relevance to the quality of social life as a whole. Whatever the 'failure' or 'success' of *Scrutiny*, however one might argue the toss between the anti-Leavisian prejudice of the literary establishment and the waspishness of the *Scrutiny* movement itself, the fact remains that English students in England today are 'Leavisites' whether they know it or not, irremediably altered by that historic intervention. There is no more need to be a card-carrying Leavisite today than there is to be a card-carrying Copernican: that current has entered the bloodstream of English studies in England as Copernicus reshaped our astronomical beliefs, has become a form of spontaneous critical wisdom as deep-seated as our conviction that the earth moves round the sun. That the 'Leavis debate' is effectively dead is perhaps the major sign of *Scrutiny*'s victory.
>
> (Eagleton 1983: 31)

This paragraph starts with a good summary of what Leavis stood for, and if Eagleton had written it at the end of a book on Leavis, it would look like a happy ending to the story told in the previous section. But it actually appears near the *beginning* of a book which is specifically an introduction to 'theory' (a very good one) and the point of it is *conversion*, signing the reader up to a different story. Like the characters at the beginning of Bunyan's *Pilgrim's Progress* who suddenly discover they are carrying a large burden of sin on their backs, Eagleton's readers need to have it pointed out to them that they are in fact 'Leavisites'. The rest of the book then takes them on a journey through all the alternatives to Leavis's approach that they were not aware of before.

The journey ends in Eagleton's book with a call to make literary study more politically conscious, and in this it reflects one of the most significant developments in the story of 'After Leavis', which is the emergence of a strong critique of Leavis from the intellectual left, led by Marxist theorists. This took a long time to get going. Leavis had always made clear his difference from Marxism, a theme he particularly emphasised in his introduction to *For Continuity* (1933), but in the 1930s, when being united against fascism was the most important thing, there had seemed to be plenty of room to combine following Leavis with a left-leaning political commitment. Leavis himself even admitted to 'believing some form of economic communism to be inevitable and desirable' (*FC* 184). After the war a more rigorously theorised critique of Leavis's politics (or lack of them) began to emerge. This started with an exploratory 'Left-Leavisism', a term particularly associated with Richard Hoggart and Raymond Williams. It took a more systematic form in the Marxist historian Perry Anderson's long essay 'Components of the National Culture', first published in 1968 in the journal *New Left Review* (behind the cover slogan 'Combat Bourgeois Ideas'). Anderson argued that British intellectual culture was incapable of producing a revolutionary politics because for various reasons it lacked a 'synthesizing discipline', a central way of understanding society as a 'totality'. He surveyed the academic discourses that had failed to produce such a discipline and concluded that only one had made a decent effort – literary criticism, as 'commanded' by Leavis. His essay thus valorised Leavis as a 'great critic' and an important figure in British culture – albeit one who had become 'banally reactionary' by the 1960s. Even so, Anderson insisted, Leavis's criticism was inadequate because, although he knew there was something wrong with British culture, he was unwilling to think of culture and society in terms of *class*. This put an 'intolerable strain' on his thinking which explained the 'displaced acrimony' of some of his polemics (Anderson 1968: 50–6). Anderson's diagnosis was taken up and developed in much more detail by other left-inclined writers, particularly research students, and a decade or so later this produced a formidable wave of critical studies of Leavis, the Arnoldian tradition, and 'English'. These studies, which included Wright (1979), Mulhern (1979), McCallum (1983), Baldick (1983) and Doyle (1989), all brought essentially the same charge against Leavis – that his criticism, however militant in tone, promoted a kind of 'substitute politics' (Wright 1979: 39); or that, as Francis Mulhern concludes, its *'logically necessary effect* was a *depreciation*, a *repression* and, at the limit, a *categorial dissolution of politics as such*' (Mulhern 1979: 330; his italics). Whether this critique was valid or not (this perhaps depends ultimately on what one recognises as 'politics') it had the additional advantage of being able to appear more serious, more radical – in a sense, more puritan – than Leavis himself. It played an important part in making Leavis's approach appear discredited and unappealing, the very opposite of the powerful effect his criticism had had on many readers in earlier decades, and in that sense it was, to recall what Eagleton says about *Scrutiny*, a 'historic intervention'.

There is still a problem, however, in determining quite how finally 'historic' such interventions have been. Mulhern's book ends by looking forward to when 'the moment of *Scrutiny* can at last be ended' (Mulhern 1979: 331) and something similar is implicit in the passage from Eagleton that I quoted before. Although Eagleton refers to '*Scrutiny's* victory', the whole point of what he is saying is to make readers question whether they want to remain subject to that victory. The hope is implied that 'theory' will eventually win its own victory over Leavis and students will make more deliberate choices about which theoretical card they bring with them to class. That was more than twenty-five years ago, of course, and Eagleton's book is still very much in print; exactly the same call is sounded to students reading it today. And yet actually, although both Mulhern and Eagleton look *forward* to an intellectual transformation, according to many other narratives it had already happened by 1983. A recent guide refers to the 'so-called theory revolution *of the 1970s*' (Waugh 2006: 3; my italics) and many of the events that figure in such narratives, such as Jacques Derrida's paper at Johns Hopkins, or the seminar series chaired by Frank Kermode in London, did indeed take place in the 1960s or 1970s. What these inconsistencies point to is that there is almost always an indeterminacy, an incompleteness, to the kind of change implied by 'after Leavis', no matter how much teachers and critics may insist critical thinking has moved on. This is not just peculiar to the question of Leavis's status, though his one-time dominance does throw it into sharper relief. It is more a feature of the way change happens (or doesn't happen) in discourses as broad in scope and loosely structured as literary studies, which no one really 'commands' in the way implied by Anderson. In this respect literary studies are quite unlike the natural sciences which, as the philosopher of science Thomas S. Kuhn famously suggested, can occasionally undergo complete transformations in their basic assumptions – 'paradigm shifts' – because of the top-down way in which authority is distributed within them and the fact that research scientists constitute a 'special kind of community' (Kuhn 1962: 166). Leavis himself thought of *Scrutiny* as bringing about permanent changes in the way literature was or ought to be studied – and was often frustrated when he came up against evidence that it hadn't happened. It was axiomatic for Leavis, for example, that the old-fashioned Shakespeare criticism of A.C. Bradley (1851–1935) was discredited and as good as dead: *Scrutiny* had effected 'the relegation of Bradley ... by bringing home to the academic world ... how inadequate and wrong the Bradley approach was' (*VC* 230). And yet Leavis had to recognise that Bradley was still what he called 'a very potent and mischievous influence' (*TCP* 137); and even in the twenty-first century Bradley is still being occasionally revisited and revalued (see Kearney 2002).

DOES LEAVIS 'EXIST'?

We need a way of thinking about living 'after Leavis' which allows for this kind of indeterminacy; and a good place to start may be the occasionally recurring trope in Leavis's criticism of the opposition between existence, or life, and non-existence. 'Eugene O'Neill doesn't exist' (Leavis 1932: 299) is a striking early example of this figure of speech, which occurs in Leavis's review of Meiklejohn's Experimental College curriculum. Leavis meant that, in his view, the American dramatist (then still alive) had not achieved anything significant enough to warrant the kind of attention he got in Meiklejohn's curriculum. His work did not 'live' in the sense that the works in the great traditions did. In *Revaluation*, similarly, Leavis was concerned to establish which of the poets of the period between Donne and Eliot could still be read as 'living'. After his attention shifted to the novel, he occasionally applied the same trope to characters: Little Dorrit was 'real' and 'unquestionably "there" for us' (DN 226), but the same could not be said for Little Nell, the tragic heroine of an earlier Dickens novel, *The Old Curiosity Shop*: 'to suggest taking Little Nell seriously would be absurd: there's nothing there' (DN 225). George Eliot's character Will Ladislaw, the romantic hero of *Middlemarch*, similarly 'can't be said to exist' (GT 75). The trope is occasionally formally revived in *The Cambridge Quarterly* where readers are presented with a passage of prose or verse which was once better known than it is now and invited to consider whether it is 'Alive or Dead?' Leavis even applied it to himself in a letter written around the time of the furore over his attack on Snow: 'There are things that everyone knows but at the same time has agreed to unknow. For the everyone of that world I both exist (to the extent of obsession) and don't exist' (IM 301).

Being prepared to take him seriously as a critical thinker in the twenty-first century entails asking the question: in his own terms, does Leavis 'exist'? Is there anything 'there' for contemporary readers to find relevant? Can we read him as a 'living' author, or is he simply a representative figure from a 'dead' past? If one surveys all the academic discourses that make up contemporary literary and cultural studies – or the more public discourses of review and discussion that surround the arts – it can seem a 'desolatingly vast' landscape and one in which Leavis is reduced to insignificance. In many ways there is no role for him in the broad agenda of modern literary studies – unless to be used for occasional target practice. In particular it is difficult to see that feminism could have anything but a critical relation with the near-invisibility of gender as an issue in Leavis's work. Psychoanalysis has a set of terms for describing what happens in texts which can make Leavis's analyses, his talk of George Eliot as a 'psychological realist', seem rather imprecise and limited in scope. And what can Leavis, preoccupied with *English* literature and the preservation of its Shakespearean qualities, contribute to post-colonial studies with its global perspective and heavily theorised narratives of the interactions of coloniser and colonised? If Leavis figures in such narratives at all, it must inevitably be on the side of the coloniser – the wrong side.

On the other hand, it is still possible to discern occasional attempts to acknowledge Leavis's relevance to contemporary debate – albeit the acknowledgment is usually heavily qualified or ironised. A good example is the phrasing of the comment by Joe Moran which I quoted in 'Key Ideas' Chapter 7: 'We obviously cannot return to Leavis's elitism ... But it is also true that ... ' A similar formula – which we might characterise as 'No, but ... ' – is also sometimes found in debates about the ethical responsibilities of literature and criticism. Thus Andrew Gibson begins his discussion of post-modernity, ethics and the novel (subtitled *From Leavis to Levinas*) by declaring that 'It is time to go back to Leavis' – but quickly reassures us that he means this 'in one (qualified) sense only' – the sense that 'novels perform an ethical work' and so one can be sympathetic to Leavis's view that 'it is worth trying to enable that work to take place' (Gibson 1999: 1). Terry Eagleton has also contributed to reconstituting the tradition of residual respect for Leavis as a flawed radical who nevertheless sets a standard for more theoretically tooled-up radicals: 'The differences are enormous, but the affinities are there' (Eagleton 1998: 49). The cultural historian Stefan Collini uses the formula 'not wholly wrong' in his analysis of Leavis's approach to cultural criticism (Collini 1998a: 173). And the Marxist critic David Simpson recognises that Leavis (with Eliot and Arnold) can still challenge contemporary practice: 'As we exhume them for their various limitations – and most histories of the discipline do this regularly – we should not gloss over the parts of their agendas that reflect on our own generational failures' (Simpson 2004: 81).

What all these 'No, but ... ' formulations suggest can perhaps be summed up as follows. After Leavis, literary studies has asked a lot of searching and valid questions that Leavis either repressed or never dreamed of – questions about language, power, class, history, post-colonialism, gender, sexuality, and so on. These dominate the agenda and determine the way literary studies thinks of itself. But some of the questions that Leavis asked still remain to be addressed – and when we do address them, we sometimes have to recognise that our questions and answers are not so different from Leavis's as we feel they ought to be. As Michael Bell suggests, Leavis 'still comes closest to expressing the impulse that leads so many people seriously to read, study, and teach literature, and he has therefore become the repressed bad conscience of the academy' (Bell 2000: 422). If this is so, it explains the way in which Leavis both exists and does not exist for contemporary critical practice – and also perhaps why references to him (like Simpson's image of *exhuming*) so often have a gothic strain to them. I suggested at the beginning of this book that to understand Leavis and his career it may be helpful to think in terms of the category of the 'monstrous' which he himself invoked several times. But to understand his continued relevance, the mode in which he continues to 'exist', we perhaps need to think in terms of a different gothic figure, that of the ghost. To think of him as a ghost is not to trivialise Leavis, but to give him back some of the power to disturb and challenge which generations of readers experienced during his life.

FURTHER READING

The best way to develop an understanding of Leavis's thought and its significance is to read more of his writings, not just the often-quoted passages that feature in introductory studies like this but the essays and books to which those passages belong. This chapter is divided into three parts. Part 1 is a guide to Leavis's books, in chronological order, concluding with a list of the chapters I would personally recommend as starting-points. Part 2 provides a guide to books about Leavis, and also recommends some recent articles. Part 3 provides some information on the bibliographical and other resources available if you want to research Leavis further.

BOOKS BY F. R. LEAVIS

New Bearings in English Poetry: A Study of the Contemporary Situation (Chatto & Windus, 1932).

Leavis's first book, which came out a few months before *Scrutiny* first appeared. The main argument is that T. S. Eliot has found a way of making poetry relevant to the modern world, but the most powerful chapter is the introductory one in which Leavis sets out clearly his view of what was so wrong with Victorian and early twentieth-century poetry that made Eliot's insights so right. There is also a long section on W. B. Yeats, and separate chapters on Pound and

Hopkins. Leavis added a postscript in 1950, still praising Eliot but deploring the influence of Auden and the other poets who had come after him.

For Continuity (Minority Press, 1933).
Leavis's first collection of essays, including almost all his contributions to the first volume of *Scrutiny*, and also his 1930 pamphlets on 'Mass Civilisation and Minority Culture' and on D. H. Lawrence. A good introduction to his early cultural criticism, though all the contents can be found elsewhere. It is also worth looking out for two other books from the same period, both introduced and edited by Leavis, which like this one were intended to maximise the impact of the early volumes of Scrutiny. *Towards Standards of Criticism* (Wishart & Co, 1933) is a selection of essays from *The Calendar of Modern Letters*, the 1920s journal on which *Scrutiny* was partly modelled; *Determinations* (Chatto & Windus, 1934) is a collection of *Scrutiny* essays by other contributors (Leavis originally wanted to call this book 'Cambridge Criticism').

[with Denys Thompson] *Culture and Environment: The Training of Critical Awareness* (Chatto & Windus, 1933).
Another book hastily compiled to give additional impetus to the *Scrutiny* 'movement', this one was designed as a resource for use in schools, particularly sixth forms, and adult education. It was widely used as a textbook and is an important document in the pre-history of 'Cultural Studies'. The first half mainly consists of a kind of workbook based on extracts from advertisements, journalism and popular fiction; the second half is mainly given over to extensive quotation from the works of George Sturt, particularly *The Wheelwright's Shop*, and D. H. Lawrence, to illustrate 'the loss of the organic community' (a chapter title). Too much reliance on *Culture and Environment* as a source for understanding Leavis tends to produce a distorted impression of him as possessed by nostalgia for a lost rural idyll. This clearly played a part in his thinking, but 'urbanity' was in many ways just as important. Leavis's co-author Denys Thompson, a school master at Gresham's School in Norfolk, was an energetic member of the original *Scrutiny* group. He later played down his contribution to *Culture and Environment* (see Thompson 1984: 48) but it is much more like other books by Thompson than like any other book by Leavis.

Revaluation: Tradition and Development in English Poetry (Chatto & Windus, 1936).
A critical survey of English poetry, starting with John Donne and ending
with Shelley and Keats. In this book Leavis effectively crossed into the
traditional domain of English literary scholarship, taking few prisoners
on the way (Milton's verse for example, is described as having 'a
wearying deadness about it' (*RV* 54)). It probably did more than any
other book in Leavis's early career to provoke hostile reaction from
within the academy and divide opinion towards him. The chapters on
Milton and on Keats are good places to study Leavis's account of the
'characteristic resources' of the English language ('the words seem to
do what they say … ' (*RV* 55)). Recently reprinted with an introduction by Paul Dean (Dean 1998; see also Dodsworth 2001).

Education and the University: A Sketch for an 'English School' (Chatto & Windus,
    1943).
Important statement of Leavis's idea of what the essential function of
a university should be, and how an 'English'-based course could fulfil it.
Also contains the text of Leavis's early pamphlet *How to Teach Reading:
A Primer for Ezra Pound* (1932). A kind of supplement to this book is
Mill on Bentham and Coleridge (Chatto & Windus, 1950) which reprints
two long essays by the philosopher John Stuart Mill which Leavis
thought would make a good resource for a study of the Victorian
period in the spirit of his 'Sketch'.

The Great Tradition: George Eliot, Henry James, Joseph Conrad (Chatto & Windus,
    1948).
For the title phrase and the provocative first chapter this has become
perhaps the best known of Leavis's books. But it is worth looking in
more detail at what Leavis actually says about his three main subjects
after the first few pages. For recent reassessments of the whole book,
see Johnson (2001) and Horne (2004).

The Common Pursuit (Chatto & Windus, 1952).
Leavis's second collection of miscellaneous essays and the one
which, in my view, best introduces his criticism. There are essays on
Eliot and Lawrence; and on a range of other key authors for Leavis,
including Pope, Bunyan, Swift, Forster and Hopkins; there are some
classic statements of Leavis's views of what criticism was and was
not (his reply to Wellek is included – see also the essays on 'Sociology
and Literature' and 'The Logic of Christian Discrimination'); and the

collection is rounded off with a fierce attack on the standards of contemporary reviewing of poetry. This book gets a bad press in several biographies of Leavis because the essays are not in chronological order and sometimes the background to each essay is not properly explained. It's easy enough to work these details out, though, and if any book can be considered the 'portable Leavis' it is probably this one.

D. H. Lawrence: Novelist (Chatto & Windus, 1955).
Based on a series of essays published under the heading 'The Novel as Dramatic Poem' in *Scrutiny* between 1950 and 1953. It should not be mistaken for a comprehensive guide to Lawrence's work, as the coverage is quite uneven. *Sons and Lovers* and *Lady Chatterley's Lover*, for example, two of Lawrence's best-known works, are dismissed in a few paragraphs; while at least half the book is given over to analysis of stories rather than full-length novels, with separate chapters on 'St Mawr', 'The Captain's Doll' and 'The Daughters of the Vicar'. The central emphasis, however, is on *The Rainbow* and *Women in Love*, and there are long chapters on both.

Two Cultures? The Significance of C. P. Snow; Being the Richmond Lecture, 1962; with an essay on Sir Charles Snow's Rede Lecture by Michael Yudkin (Chatto & Windus, 1962).
The text of Leavis's famous attack on Snow, though for a full sense of its impact and the public debate it provoked it is better to look through a bound volume of *The Spectator* where it was originally published in March 1962; or in *Nor Shall My Sword* (see below 1972). This edition of the text is mainly of interest for the addition of an essay by a young Cambridge scientist, Michael Yudkin, also critical of Snow's pretensions to speak for science (this tactic of co-opting a friendly scientist anticipates Leavis's later use of Michael Polanyi as an ally in his attack on philosophy). For the background to Leavis's attack on Snow see Collini (1998b) and Ortolano (2005, 2009).

A Selection from Scrutiny (2 vols: Cambridge University Press, 1968).
A selection compiled by Leavis himself, and organised according to his headings. Not fully representative, as he admits, because it is focused on English literature and does not include any essays on music or European writing – but useful for getting a sense of the other work that appeared alongside Leavis's in *Scrutiny* (particularly Q. D. Leavis's essays and reviews, which are well represented).

'Anna Karenina' and Other Essays (Chatto & Windus, 1967).

Leavis's third collection of miscellaneous essays; and as the title suggests this one has a bit more of an international flavour than *For Continuity* or *The Common Pursuit*. Besides the essay on the classic Russian novel *Anna Karenina* (in choosing this topic Leavis was following Arnold and Lawrence) many of the essays collected are on American authors. Other essays are mainly on topics familiar from earlier books: George Eliot, T. S. Eliot, Bunyan, Conrad, Lawrence. The final essay, 'The Orthodoxy of Enlightenment', is Leavis's comment on the Lady Chatterley trial (1960).

[With Q. D. Leavis] *Lectures in America* (Chatto & Windus, 1969).

The text of three lectures by F. R. Leavis, and one long essay based on several lectures by Q. D. Leavis, given at Cornell and Harvard Universities, USA, in October 1966. Q. D. Leavis's powerful essay on *Wuthering Heights* (still often reprinted or quoted in textbooks on this novel) is a good example of her characteristic methods and manner. Of the three lectures by F. R. Leavis, the first two are variations on familiar themes (C. P. Snow and T. S. Eliot). The third, 'Yeats: The Problem and the Challenge', is the most interesting (for a detailed analysis of this lecture see Bell 1988: 74–83).

English Literature in Our Time and the University: The Clark Lectures, 1967 (Chatto & Windus, 1969).

Not to be confused with *Education and the University* (see above 1943), this book reprints the Clark Lectures which Leavis was invited to give in Cambridge in 1967 (though a photograph of the University of York was pointedly used for the cover illustration). All Leavis's preoccupations in the 1960s are synthesised here – Eliot, Lawrence, English, the university, 'technologico-Benthamism' – and it is a good source of typical pronouncements on all these topics, though the lectures themselves contain little that is not found elsewhere in Leavis's books. The book is most worth consulting for the introductory essay, in which Leavis tells his own version of the story of the origins of 'Cambridge English'.

[With Q. D. Leavis] *Dickens the Novelist* (Chatto & Windus, 1970).

Q.D. Leavis's is the dominant voice in this book. She contributed four substantial essays and some other notes. F. R. Leavis contributed three chapters, one an extended version of the essay on *Hard Times* which had already appeared in *The Great Tradition*; one a previously published introduction to *Dombey and Son*; and one (for which this book is most worth reading) a substantial new essay on *Little Dorrit*.

Nor Shall My Sword: Discourses on Pluralism, Compassion and Social Hope (Chatto & Windus, 1972).

The text (in at least one case substantially revised) of six lectures given by Leavis between 1962 and 1971, starting with the Richmond Lecture. The best introduction to this most polemical period in Leavis's career. The subtitle is an ironic reference to statements by two of his main targets, Lord Snow and Lord Annan.

Letters in Criticism. Edited by John Tasker (Chatto & Windus, 1974).

A very useful collection of most (67) of Leavis's published letters to the press between 1932 and 1973. Browsing through this book is a good way of sampling Leavis's approach to public debate and controversy, although for a more detailed study it is best to look up the letters in their original context (usually a weekly newspaper or periodical). It should also be noted that the satirical headings which appear over each letter in this book were devised by the editor and are not always the titles under which the letters originally appeared.

The Living Principle: 'English' as a Discipline of Thought (Chatto & Windus, 1975).

Recently reprinted (Dean 1998). For some this is the most powerful and 'philosophical' of Leavis's later books – see my 'Key Ideas' Chapter 2, for an account of the first two chapters. The third and final chapter, on T. S. Eliot's 'Four Quartets', is probably only of interest to those who want to follow every last twist and turn in Leavis's career-long dialogue with himself about Eliot. There are plenty of other essays which are a better introduction to this relationship – particularly in *The Common Pursuit*.

Thought, Words and Creativity: Art and Thought in Lawrence (Chatto & Windus, 1976).

Least known or read of all Leavis's books, and not a good one to start with. It develops the ideas outlined in the 'Language, Thought and Objectivity' chapter of *The Living Principle* and applies them to four Lawrence texts. Most interesting perhaps for extended discussion of *The Plumed Serpent*, which Leavis had avoided before. A good summary of the argument can be found in Ferns (2000).

The Critic as Anti-Philosopher: Essays and Papers by F. R. Leavis. Edited by G. Singh (Chatto & Windus, 1982).

Valuation in Criticism and other essays. Edited by G. Singh (Cambridge University Press, 1986).

These two books, edited by Leavis's friend and literary executor, bring together many of the published essays and introductions that Leavis did not get round to collecting and republishing before his death (he was apparently working on the volume which became *The Critic as Anti-Philosopher* before he fell ill in 1977). *Valuation in Criticism* also includes three previously unpublished works (probably given as lectures) 'T. S. Eliot's Influence', 'Standards of Criticism', and 'Thought, Meaning and Sensibility'; also some fragmentary 'Notes on Wordsworth'.

WHERE TO START

The Common Pursuit is the best book to start with. From the other books I would personally recommend the following essays as starting-points:

1. 'Poetry and the Modern World' in *New Bearings in English Poetry.*
2. 'Mass Civilisation and Minority Culture' in *For Continuity* (also in later editions of *Education and the University*).
3. 'Marxism and Cultural Continuity' in *For Continuity* (also in *Valuation in Criticism*).
4. 'Keats' in *Revaluation.*
5. 'Literary Studies' in *Education and the University.*
6. 'The Great Tradition' in *The Great Tradition.*
7. 'Lawrence and Class: "The Daughters of the Vicar"' in *D. H. Lawrence: Novelist.*
8. 'The Americanness of American Literature' in '*Anna Karenina and Other Essays*'.
9. 'Two Cultures? The Significance of C. P. Snow' in *Nor Shall My Sword.*
10. 'Thought, Language and Objectivity' in *The Living Principle.*
11. 'Memories of Wittgenstein' in *The Critic as Anti-Philosopher.*
12. 'Wordsworth: The Creative Conditions' in *The Critic as Anti-Philosopher.*

BOOKS ABOUT LEAVIS

Bell, Michael (1988) *F. R. Leavis,* London: Routledge.

Notable for chapter on 'Language, Truth and Literature' which explores parallels between Leavis and Heidegger. Bell has done more than any other writer on Leavis to locate his thought in a European philosophical tradition (see also Bell 1997, 1999, 2000, 2007).

Day, Gary (1996) *Re-Reading Leavis*, Basingstoke: Macmillan.
Quite unlike any other study of Leavis, this stimulating book attempts three different things at once: it relentlessly deconstructs some of Leavis's key terms and figures of speech, particularly the economic metaphors; it juxtaposes Leavis with a wide range of continental theorists, suggesting unexpected affinities as well as differences; and it reaffirms the importance of Leavis as a thinker and critic. The first two projects tend to overwhelm the last, but the book certainly delivers a lot of new insights, particularly on 'Mass Civilisation and Minority Culture' and *Culture and Environment*. See also Day 2006, 2008.

Ferns, John (2000) *F. R. Leavis*, New York: Twayne Publishers.
Contains very little in the way of critical reflection on the possibility that anyone might ever disagree with Leavis, but does provide useful summaries of all the books and is crammed with quotations.

MacKillop, Ian (1995) *F. R. Leavis: A Life in Criticism*, London: Allen Lane/ The Penguin Press.
Far more extensively researched than any other biographical study of Leavis, this is an essential source for details of Leavis's life and career, correcting many earlier misrepresentations. Ian MacKillop was himself a student of Leavis at Downing at the end of the 1950s, and his biography was generally regarded as successful in its sympathetic but even-handed treatment of the many controversial episodes in Leavis's life; but for more on this it is also well worth reading the special issue of the *Cambridge Quarterly* (1996) which consisted entirely of a symposium on the MacKillop biography (see also Mencher 1998 for a kind of counter-symposium). For some new information on aspects of Leavis's career see Alloway (2003).

MacKillop, Ian, and Richard Storer (eds.) (1995) *F. R. Leavis: Essays and Documents*, Sheffield: Sheffield Academic Press.
A miscellany of material, designed to complement the 1995 biography; includes memoirs from different periods in Leavis's career, notes and documents from Leavis's teaching, and an account of his attempt in the 1970s to republish *Daniel Deronda* as 'Gwendolen Harleth'.

Mulhern, Francis (1979) *The Moment of 'Scrutiny'*, London: New Left Books.
A powerful and searching critique of Leavis's thought – even if you are
not susceptible to the logic of Marxist/materialist critique, it is still
invaluable as a study of the whole discourse of *Scrutiny*, not just Leavis's
essays but those of the other contributors (in the 1930s a more diverse
group than is often realised). The analyses of Leavis's exchanges with
Wellek (162–76) and Bateson (297–302), and the final chapter, 'Scrutiny
in Retrospect', are essential reading. It is also well worth looking at
Mulhern's later essays on Leavis (see Mulhern 1990, 1995, 2000).

Samson, Anne (1992) *F. R. Leavis*, Hemel Hempstead: Harvester Wheatsheaf.
A lone female voice on this list, Anne Samson follows Michael Bell in
seeking to affirm Leavis's values but put them in a broader perspective –
in this case with an interesting element of personal testimony added at
certain points. Contains sensible and perceptive comments on almost
every Leavis-related topic. A good example perhaps of a dialogue with
Leavis that takes seriously his invitation to respond 'Yes, but … '.

Singh, G. (1995) *F. R. Leavis: A Literary Biography*, London: Duckworth.
Rather like Ferns (see above) but there are no references for the quotations.
Very useful, however, in that the author (one of Leavis's literary
executors) quotes extensively from otherwise unpublished material – Q. D.
Leavis's memoir of her husband, and Leavis's letters to Singh and to his
publisher.

Thompson, Denys (ed.) (1984) *The Leavises: Recollections and Impressions*,
   Cambridge: Cambridge University Press.
The best collection of memoirs, including contributions from some
key figures in Leavis's career; particularly notable for Raymond Williams's memoir 'Seeing a Man Running'.

Watson, Garry (1977) *The Leavises, The 'Social' & The Left*, Swansea: Brynmill.
Highly polemical book claiming that the Leavises' criticism has never
been taken seriously by the literary and academic worlds and this
accounts for the 'shoddy thinking' and 'failure of nerve' which characterise English culture.

Other books you may come across are Hayman (1976), Boyers (1978),
Greenwood (1978), Bilan (1979), Walsh (1980) and Robertson (1981).
These books contain some insightful comment and reflection, but look
rather dated and lacking in critical edge alongside Mulhern (1979).

OTHER RESOURCES

It is worth bearing in mind that most of the chapters in Leavis's books were originally published separately as articles in a different (often more 'embattled') context; some republished essays were substantially changed from their original form; and some of Leavis's essays remain unrepublished to this day. It is good academic practice to track some of these texts back to their original context, and a lot of the hard work has already been done for you, by several generations of bibliographers. The Garland Annotated Bibliography for the Leavises, compiled by William Baker, Maurice Kinch and John Kimber (Baker 1989) is a fantastic resource, which lists all Leavis's publications and republications and provides a short summary of the content of every text it lists. It also provides an extensive listing of writings about the Leavises up to 1984, and is comprehensively indexed. Before this came along there was McKenzie and Allum's 'Checklist' (McKenzie and Allum 1966) which only covers up to the mid-sixties but is still valuable as it provides one chronological listing of all Leavis's publications, year-by-year, whereas the Garland has one list for books, one for articles, one for letters, etc. One other bibliographical resource to note is my own list, derived from the Garland, of the articles that remained uncollected at Leavis's death (Storer 1995b).

Many university libraries still have a set of the twenty-volume reprint of *Scrutiny*; and the individual volumes are also now available in paperback from Cambridge University Press.

A copy of Leavis's unpublished PhD thesis, 'The Relationship of Journalism to Literature: Studied in the Rise and Earlier Development of the Press in England' (1924), is accessible in the Cambridge University Library. The thesis is discussed in some detail by Ferns (2000) and Alloway (2003).

Besides the letters he wrote for publication (see *LC*) Leavis kept up a very large private correspondence with former students, colleagues, associates, editors and others. These are essentially business letters, but often include memorable or mildly scandalous asides on whatever issue or controversy Leavis was preoccupied with at the time of writing, together with occasional references to more personal concerns. They do not – as far as I am aware – reveal a completely different side to Leavis, but do provide an interesting gloss on what is already known. It has been suggested that Leavis wrote 'something like half a dozen letters a day' (*IM* xv) and if this estimate should turn out to be even only half true it would mean that Leavis wrote over 50,000 letters during his career. As many of these letters will have been prized and kept by their recipients it is likely that numerous small collections of letters will eventually make their way, if not into print, at least into the semi-public domain of libraries and archives – as indeed many already have. The largest collection of Leavis correspondence in the UK at the moment is held as part of the Chatto & Windus and Bodley Head archives in the University of Reading Library. A number of Cambridge colleges and libraries also hold small collections of Leavis letters and other papers. In the USA, an important collection of letters from Leavis to the poet Ronald Bottrall is held by the Harry Ransom Center in Texas. Many other letters remain in private hands but a large number were made available to the late Ian MacKillop for his research and are occasionally quoted from in his biography of Leavis. Over one hundred folders of papers and documents accumulated in the course of Ian MacKillop's research for this biography were deposited with the University of Sheffield Library (Special Collections) after his death.

WORKS CITED

Alloway, Ross (2003) 'Selling the Great Tradition: Resistance and Conformity in the Publishing Practices of F. R. Leavis', *Book History*, 6: 227–50.

Anderson, Perry (1968) 'Components of the National Culture', *New Left Review,* 50: 3–57.

Arnold, Matthew (1965) *The Complete Prose Works of Matthew Arnold Volume 5: Culture and Anarchy with Friendship's Garland and Some Literary Essays*, in R. H. Super (ed.), Ann Arbor: University of Michigan Press.

Baker, William, Kinch, Maurice and Kimber, John (1989) *F. R. Leavis and Q. D. Leavis: An Annotated Bibliography*, New York: Garland.

Baldick, Chris (1983) *The Social Mission of English Criticism 1848–1932*, Oxford: Clarendon Press.

Ball, Stephen (1987) 'English for the English since 1906', in Ivor Goodson (ed.), *Social Histories of the Secondary Curriculum: Subjects for Study*, London: Falmer Press.

Barry, Peter (1995) *Beginning Theory: An Introduction to Literary and Cultural Theory*, Manchester: Manchester University Press.

Bateson, F. W. (1953a) 'The Function of Criticism at the Present Time', *Essays in Criticism*, 3: 1–27.

——(1953b) 'Correspondence: The Responsible Critic', *Scrutiny*, 19.4: 317–21.

Bell, Michael (1988) *F. R. Leavis*, London: Routledge.

——(1997) 'The Afterlife of F. R. Leavis: Dead but Won't Lie Down', *The Cambridge Quarterly*, 26: 196–9.

——(1999) 'What Price Collaboration? The Case of F. R. Leavis', in Dominic Rainsford and Tim Wood (eds), *Critical Ethics: Text, Theory and Responsibility*, Basingstoke: Macmillan.

——(2000) 'F. R. Leavis', in A. Walton Litz, Louis Menand and Lawrence Rainey (eds), *Cambridge History of Literary Criticism Vol 7: Modernism and the New Criticism*, Cambridge: Cambridge University Press.

——(2007) *Open Secrets: Literature, Education and Authority from J-J. Rousseau to J.M. Coetzee*, Oxford: Oxford University Press.

Belsey, Catherine (1982) 'Re-reading the great tradition', in Peter Widdowson (ed.), *Re-Reading English,* London: Methuen.

Bergonzi, Bernard (1984) 'Leavis and Eliot: The Long Road to Rejection', *Critical Quarterly*, 26: 21–43.

Bilan, R. B. (1979) *The Literary Criticism of F. R. Leavis*, Cambridge: Cambridge University Press.

Black, Michael (1975) 'A Kind of Valediction: Leavis on Eliot 1929–75', *New Universities Quarterly*, 30: 78–93.

Boyers, Robert (1978) *F. R. Leavis: Judgment and the Discipline of Thought*, London: University of Missouri Press.

Collini, Stefan (1998a) 'The Critic as Journalist: Leavis after *Scrutiny*', in Jeremy Treglown and Bridget Bennett (eds), *Grub Street and Ivory Tower: Literary Journalism and Literary Scholarship from Fielding to the Internet*, Oxford: Clarendon Press.

——(1998b) 'Introduction' to C. P. Snow, *The Two Cultures*, Cambridge: Cambridge University Press.

Cullen, Barry (1993) '"I thought I had provided something better" – F. R. Leavis, Literary Criticism and Anti-Philosophy', in Gary Day (ed.), *The British Critical Tradition: A Re-evaluation*, Basingstoke: Macmillan.

Davies, Tony (1997) *Humanism*, London: Routledge.

Day, Gary (1996) *Re-Reading Leavis: Culture and Literary Criticism*, Basingstoke: Macmillan.

——(2006) 'F. R. Leavis: Criticism and Culture', in Patricia Waugh (ed.), *Literary Theory and Criticism: An Oxford Guide*, Oxford: Oxford University Press.

——(2008) *Literary Criticism: A New History*, Edinburgh: Edinburgh University Press.

Dean, Paul (1998) *Introduction to F. R. Leavis, The Living Principle: 'English' as a Discipline of Thought*, Chicago: Ivan R. Dee, Elephant Paperbacks.

Derrida, Jacques (2003), 'Following Theory', in John Schad and Michael Payne (eds), *Life.After.Theory*, London: Continuum.

Dodsworth, Martin (2001) 'Coercive Suggestion: Rhetoric and Community in *Revaluation*', in Maureen Bell *et al.* (eds), *Reconstructing the Book: Literary Texts in Transmission*, Aldershot: Ashgate.

Doyle, Brian (1989) *English and Englishness*, London: Routledge.

Eagleton, Terry (1983) *Literary Theory: An Introduction*, Oxford: Blackwell.

——(1998) 'Revaluations: F. R. Leavis', *The European English Messenger*, 7.2: 49–51.

Eliot, T. S. (1931) [untitled review of J. M. Murry, *Son of Woman: The Story of D. H. Lawrence*] *The Criterion*, 10: 768–74.

——(1953) *Selected Prose*, in John Hayward (ed.), Harmondsworth: Penguin.

Ferns, John (2000) *F. R. Leavis*, New York: Twayne.

Ford, Boris (1984) 'Round and about the *Pelican Guide to English Literature*', in Denys Thompson (ed.), *The Leavises: Recollections and Impressions*, Cambridge: Cambridge University Press.

Gibson, Andrew (1999) *Postmodernity, Ethics and the Novel: from Leavis to Levinas*, London: Routledge.

Greenwood, Edward (1978) *F. R. Leavis*, Harlow: Longman.

Hawkes, Terence (1992) *Meaning by Shakespeare*, London: Routledge.

Hawkins, Harriet (1990) *Classics and Trash: Traditions and Taboos in High Literature and Popular Modern Genres*, Toronto: University of Toronto Press.

Hayman, Ronald (1976) *Leavis*, London: Heinemann.

Horne, Philip (2004) 'New Impressions VI: F. R. Leavis and *The Great Tradition*', *Essays in Criticism*, 54: 165–80.

'Ille Ego' (1933) 'Readers and Writers', *New English Weekly*, 5 January, 282–3.

Jameson, Storm (1970) *Journey from the North II*, London: Collins and Harvill.

Johnson, Claudia L. (2001) 'F. R. Leavis: The "Great Tradition" of the English Novel and the Jewish Part', *Nineteenth-Century Literature*, 56: 198–227.

Joyce, Chris (2005) 'Meeting in Meaning: Philosophy and Theory in the Work of F. R. Leavis', *Modern Age*, 47.3: 240–9.

Kearney, Anthony (1989) 'Leavis on Eliot: Personality versus Intelligence', *The Use of English*, 40.3: 59–67.

——(2002) 'A Mischievous Influence: Leavis on Bradley on Shakespeare', *The Use of English*, 54.2: 140–7.

Keynes, Geoffrey (ed.) (1966) *Blake: Complete Writings*, Oxford: Oxford University Press.

Kuhn, Thomas S. (1962) *The Structure of Scientific Revolutions*, Chicago: University of Chicago Press.

Lawford, Paul (1976) 'Conservative Empiricism in Literary Theory: A Scrutiny of the Work of F. R. Leavis', *Red Letters*, 1: 12–15; 2: 9–11.

Lawrence, D. H. (1986) *The Rainbow*, Harmondsworth: Penguin.

Leavis, F. R. (1932) 'An American Lead', *Scrutiny*, 1.3: 297–300.

——(1934) 'Why Universities?', *Scrutiny*, 3.2: 117–32.

——(1939) 'Arnold's Thought', *Scrutiny*, 8.1: 92–9.

——(1942) 'After "To The Lighthouse"', *Scrutiny*, 10.3: 295–8.

——(1950) *Mill on Bentham and Coleridge*, London: Chatto & Windus.

——(1951) 'The Legacy of the "Twenties"', *The Listener*, 29 March, 502–3.

——(1953a) 'The Responsible Critic: or The Function of Criticism at Any Time', *Scrutiny*, 19.3: 162–83.

——(1953b) 'Correspondence: The Responsible Critic', *Scrutiny*, 19.4: 321–8.

———(1976) *Thought, Words and Creativity: Art and Thought in Lawrence*, London: Chatto & Windus.

MacCabe, Colin (1978) *James Joyce and the Revolution of the Word*, London: Macmillan.

MacKillop, Ian (1995) 'Rubrics and Reading Lists', in Ian MacKillop and Richard Storer (eds), *F. R. Leavis: Essays and Documents*, Sheffield: Sheffield Academic Press.

Martin, Graham (1996) 'Critical Opinion: F. R. Leavis and the Function of Criticism', *Essays in Criticism*, 66.1: 1–15.

Matthews, Sean (1997) '"Rotten and Rotting Others" – D. H. Lawrence and English Studies', *Studies in English Language and Literature*, 47: 39–63.

———(2004) 'The Responsibilities of Dissent: F. R. Leavis after *Scrutiny*', *Literature and History*, 13.2: 49–66.

McCallum, Pamela (1983) *Literature and Method: Towards a Critique of I. A. Richards, T. S. Eliot and F. R. Leavis*, Dublin: Gill & Macmillan.

McIlroy, John (1993) 'Teacher, Critic, Explorer', in W. John Morgan and Peter Preston (eds), *Raymond Williams: Politics, Education, Letters*, Basingstoke: Palgrave Macmillan.

McKenzie, D. F. and Allum, M.-P. (1966) *F. R. Leavis: a Check-list 1924–1964*, London: Chatto & Windus.

Meiklejohn, Alexander (2001) *The Experimental College*, Madison: University of Wisconsin Press.

Mencher, M. B. (ed.) (1998) *Leavis, Dr MacKillop and The Cambridge Quarterly*, Harleston: The Brynmill Press.

Milner, Andrew (1994) *Contemporary Cultural Theory: An Introduction*, London: UCL Press.

Montefiore, Jan and Varney, Kate (2008) 'A Conversation About Q. D. Leavis', *Women: A Cultural Review*, 19.2: 172–87.

Moran, Joe (2002) 'F. R. Leavis, English and the University', *English*, 51.199: 1–13.

Mulhern, Francis (1979) *The Moment of 'Scrutiny'*, London: NLB.

———(1990) 'English Reading', in Homi K. Bhabha (ed.), *Nation and Narration*, London: Routledge.

———(1995) 'Culture and Authority', *Critical Quarterly*, 37.1: 77–89.

———(2000) *Culture/Metaculture*, London: Routledge.

Nelson, Adam R. (2001) *Education and Democracy: The Meaning of Alexander Meiklejohn 1872–1964*, Madison: University of Wisconsin Press.

Newton, K. M. (1992) *Theory into Practice: A Reader in Modern Literary Criticism*, Basingstoke: Macmillan.

Ortolano, Guy (2005) 'F. R. Leavis, Science, and the Abiding Crisis of Modern Civilization', *History of Science*, 43: 161–85.

———(2009) *The Two Cultures Controversy: Science, Literature and Cultural Politics in Postwar Britain*, Cambridge: Cambridge University Press.

Page, Charles (1995) '"Cunning Passages": Leavis's Lectures on Poetry and Prose', in Ian MacKillop and Richard Storer (eds), *F. R. Leavis: Essays and Documents*, Sheffield: Sheffield Academic Press.

Paige, D. D. (ed.) (1950) *The Selected Letters of Ezra Pound 1907–1941*, London: Faber & Faber.

Poole, Roger (1996) [untitled] in 'F. R. Leavis Special Issue: Reminiscences and Revaluations', *The Cambridge Quarterly*, 25: 391–5.

Robertson, P. J. M. (1981) *The Leavises on Fiction: An Historic Partnership*, London: Macmillan.

Samson, Anne (1992) *F. R. Leavis*, Hemel Hempstead: Harvester Wheatsheaf.

Schad, John (2003) 'Epilogue: Coming Back to "Life": "Leavis spells pianos"', in John Schad and Michael Payne (eds), *Life.After.Theory*, London: Continuum.

Selden, Raman (1989) *Practising Theory and Reading Literature: An Introduction*, Hemel Hempstead: Harvester Wheatsheaf.

Simpson, David (2004) 'Politics as Such?', *New Left Review*, 30: 69–82.

Snow, C. P. (1970) 'The Case of Leavis and the Serious Case', *Times Literary Supplement*, 9 July, 737–40.

Stewart, Stanley (2003) 'Was Wittgenstein a Closet Literary Critic?', *New Literary History*, 34: 43–57.

Stewart, Victoria (2004) 'Q.D Leavis: Women and Education under Scrutiny', *Literature and History*, 13.2: 67–85.

Storer, Richard (1995a) 'F. R. Leavis and the Idea of a University', *The Cambridge Review*, 116: 94–100.

——(1995b) 'F. R. Leavis: A Reader's Guide', in Ian MacKillop and Richard Storer (eds), *F. R. Leavis: Essays and Documents*, Sheffield: Sheffield Academic Press.

Thompson, Denys (ed.) (1984) *The Leavises: Recollections and Impressions*, Cambridge: Cambridge University Press.

Tillyard, E. M. W. (1958) *The Muse Unchained: An Intimate Account of the Revolution in English Studies at Cambridge*, London: Bowes & Bowes.

Trilling, Lionel (1966) *Beyond Culture*, London: Secker & Warburg.

Walsh, William (1980) *F. R. Leavis*, London: Chatto & Windus.

Waugh, Patricia (2006) 'Introduction: Criticism, Theory, and Anti-theory', in Patricia Waugh (ed.), *Literary Theory and Criticism: An Oxford Guide*, Oxford: Oxford University Press.

Wellek, René (1937a) 'Literary Criticism and Philosophy', *Scrutiny*, 5: 375–83.

——(1937b) 'Correspondence: Literary Criticism and Philosophy', *Scrutiny*, 6: 195–6.

Williams, Raymond (1959) 'Our Debt to Dr Leavis', *The Critical Quarterly*, 1.3: 245–7.

——(1961) *Culture and Society 1780–1950*, Harmondsworth: Penguin.

Wright, Iain (1979) 'F. R. Leavis, the *Scrutiny* movement and the Crisis', in Jonathan Clark *et al.* (eds), *Culture and Crisis in Britain in the Thirties*, London: Lawrence and Wishart.

INDEX

eBooks – at www.eBookstore.tandf.co.uk

A library at your fingertips!

eBooks are electronic versions of printed books. You can store them on your PC/laptop or browse them online.

They have advantages for anyone needing rapid access to a wide variety of published, copyright information.

eBooks can help your research by enabling you to bookmark chapters, annotate text and use instant searches to find specific words or phrases. Several eBook files would fit on even a small laptop or PDA.

NEW: Save money by eSubscribing: cheap, online access to any eBook for as long as you need it.

Annual subscription packages

We now offer special low-cost bulk subscriptions to packages of eBooks in certain subject areas. These are available to libraries or to individuals.

For more information please contact webmaster.ebooks@tandf.co.uk

We're continually developing the eBook concept, so keep up to date by visiting the website.

www.eBookstore.tandf.co.uk

Made in the USA
Middletown, DE
28 April 2022